# ROCK 'N' ROLL
# EXTERMINATOR

THE

# ROCK 'N' ROLL EXTERMINATOR

## A HIP AND HAPPENING GUIDE TO GETTING RID OF RATS, MICE, BUGS, AND OTHER ANNOYING CREATURES

CAROLINE KNECHT

ILLUSTRATED BY
JED COLLINS

SKYHORSE PUBLISHING

Skyhorse Publishing books may be purchased in bulk at special discounts for sales promotion, corporate gifts, fund-raising, or educational purposes. Special editions can also be created to specifications. For details, contact the Special Sales Department, Skyhorse Publishing, 307 West 36th Street, 11th Floor, New York, NY 10018 or info@skyhorsepublishing.com.

Skyhorse® and Skyhorse Publishing® are registered trademarks of Skyhorse Publishing, Inc.®, a Delaware corporation.

Visit our website at www.skyhorsepublishing.com.

10 9 8 7 6 5 4 3 2 1

Library of Congress Cataloging-in-Publication Data is available on file.

ISBN: 978-1-62873-641-0

Printed in the United States of America

FOR DG.

# Table of Contents

# Introduction:
# How to Use This Book

This is a book about how to catch pests in your home—not the human kind like parents, in-laws, or college roommates (but if you've seen such a guide, please let us know). This book is about the kind of creepy critters that eat all your good munchies, live in your bathtub, poop all over your kitchen counters, or feast on your blood while you're sleeping.

This project started with a group of friends sharing terrifying encounters with mice, and we quickly learned that we were not alone. (It always helps to know you're in good company.) Everyone has a freaky pest story to tell. We live in New York City, so we probably have more than most. This makes us budding experts and ideal authorities on dealing with all kinds of disgusting creatures (human and non-human alike). WE LIVE THIS SHIT! But obviously we know not everyone lives in New York, so we've tried to be as inclusive as possible. Country folk and suburbanites can use these tips, too, because poison is poison. Whatever kills a city mouse will kill a country mouse.

Pests aren't just a problem for dirty people. Even the neatest of neat freaks will have to kill a cockroach at least once, and having bedbugs doesn't mean you are living in squalor, no matter what your mother heard on *The Today Show*.

We'll teach you all kinds of badass ways to snuff out mice, rats, cockroaches, bedbugs, spiders, and more. For the soft at heart, we'll go over ways to get rid of pests without killing them, but we firmly believe that the key to a pest-free life is total annihilation at all costs. Shoot to kill, baby. Shoot. To. Kill. This means there's a lot of death in this book, so if you are an activist or a keeper of pet rats, this is probably not the book for you.

Like any group of young(ish) people living in

New York City, we are very poor. We can't afford exterminators, and most of our landlords are scumbags who won't spring for it, so we have to take matters into our own hands. We are the true vigilantes of the war on pests! All of the methods in this book are tailor-made for the tightest of budgets. Most of them use ingredients you probably already have in your cupboard, and whatever you don't have you can buy for super cheap (or you can steal it).

We've tried to make this book as fun as possible, making it easy for you to become deeply engrossed in the enthralling world of pest-control.

So grab a beer and a shotgun and buckle up. You're in for the ride of your life.

# CHAPTER ONE:
# MICE

A mouse in the house is a rite of passage. No matter where you've moved from, you'll feel downright citified when you see that furry little beast scurry across your kitchen floor for the first time. It can be a very traumatic experience. (Some say it can bring a grown man to tears.) But panicking isn't going to get you anywhere, and neither is locking yourself in your room. Feel the fear! Harness it! You can channel it later when waging war.

Nobody really knows whether mice or cockroaches are the most common city pest. Both are an inevitable reality of city life, and most people would rather have one or the other. But the truth is, you'll probably have both.

Country mice are the hillbillies of the pest world. They aren't as used to humans as city mice are, and they usually roam the prairies in search of scraps of food, suitable mates, and moonshine. They are often scrappier and less refined than their uppity city cousins, but remember: what kills a city mouse kills a country mouse, too.

## Hobbies

Mice enjoy chewing on things, scurrying, eating, and having sex.

## Love Lives

Mice love doing it. Some people say there are as many mice in the world as there are humans (that's about five billion), but that is probably a myth. Lady mice can start having babies as early as two months old, but getting preggers so early is hard on their little mice bodies. We've heard all kinds of estimates, but it seems house mice give birth about six to ten times a year, and if each litter can contain four to nine babies, that's about ninety mice a year. Not even Mormons have that many kids! Think of the stretch marks.

There is no breeding season. Mice get it on whenever they damn well please.

Mice can't drive expensive cars, and they don't have a knowledge of fine wines or jazz music, so they are forced to seduce babes the only way they

If female mice spend a lot of time together in close quarters, they will lose the urge to breed altogether. However, once they get a whiff of male mouse pee, they go totally bone crazy. Then they're usually knocked up within 72 hours.

know how: by screeching and gnawing. Ladies love a high-pitched, ultrasonic call, and when a chick sees a dude with giant yellow teeth, she knows he's big and strong and able to provide, so she'll give him a ton of babies.

## Social Lives

City mice have what is called a *commensal relationship* with humans. This means that they benefit from our existence, but we do not benefit from theirs at all. They just take, take, take! Commensal mice usually have an excess food supply because they are hoarding all the crumbs your roommate didn't clean up after he made dinner. Male mice get super aggressive and territorial when there is a surplus of food, but the females play nicer and don't kill

their babies as often. (Infanticide is common among mice when food supplies are skimpy.)

Country mice are non-commensal, which basically means they mooch off us less than city mice do. They are scrappier than the wimpy, spoiled mice in the city. Field mice have a harder time finding food in the wild, so aggression levels in both sexes are much higher. They will cut a bitch for some food. Mice don't like cold or snow (who does?!), and a winter-

time shortage of insects and seeds causes them to look for warmer, safer climates, like your silverware drawer. Winter is the best time to control mice, since numbers are scarce and morale is low. Although they are not seasonal breeders, they have been known to get a little horny around March, so if you can take 'em out in the wintertime you might be able to keep them from multiplying come spring.

# Diseases

Mice carry all sorts of gnarly diseases. The fumes from their dried up poop can mess with your allergies and aggravate your asthma. You could also catch a terrifying deadly disease like one of these:

HANTAVIRUS!

Hantavirus is an infection of the lungs. Humans become infected by inhaling toxic airborne particles spread by mouse pee, poop, and spit. Symptoms are pretty much those of your standard flu (chills, puking, fever, etc.), and within a few days you start to experience difficulty breathing, a drop in blood pressure, and kidney failure. There is no treatment, and it's fatal almost half the time. But don't worry! It's pretty rare. Only about six hundrd cases have been reported in the United States since 1993.

## TULAREMIA!

Also called *rabbit fever*. This one is an extremely infectious bacterial disease! It's most often transmitted by rabbits (so it's not just a clever name), but mice are carriers as well. Like with Hantavirus, you get rabbit fever by inhaling the infected poop particles. You can also get it from a bite. If you get bitten by an infected mouse, you'll get these disgusting pustules or skin ulcers, like a leper.

This is the stuff nightmares are made of: Mice were found eating some lady's face in a nursing home in Canada. The poor old thing had dementia, so she had no idea what was going on. Thank God the nurse walked in or she could have been nothing but a pile of bones by morning. Thankfully, she wasn't hurt. But she has been "emotionally impacted" by the incident. Duh!

There are about two hundred cases of tularemia reported each year in the United States, with cases popping up in every state except Hawaii. Symptoms include chills, fever, headache, cough, diarrhea, swollen glands, and being a weaker, lazier piece of shit than you already are. And also those disgusting skin ulcers.

## RICKETTSIALPOX!

Transmitted by the mites that feed on infected mice. If you get bit by an infected mite, you'll get a bump that turns into a nasty black scab. Then a few days later you'll get the standard flu symptoms: fever, chills, aches, blah blah blah. You'll also probably develop a rash. People who live in the city have a higher chance of catching this one. It was discovered after, like, a whole apartment building in Queens started reporting symptoms. Poor Queens!

## BUBONIC PLAUGE!

The plague is the coolest of all the diseases you can get from rodents. See page 75 for more.

# How to Tell If You Have Mice

It's not rocket science. You'll know. You'll hear them scratching around in your walls, and you'll notice that all your Fritos have been ripped open and scattered around. You might even hear the shrill cries of a midnight mouse orgy. But if none of these apply (or you're just really dumb), there are other things to look for:

- Little Tiny Tracks

Maybe your kitchen counter is covered in so much grime that you'll notice a trail of tiny footprints. Or, if you're suspicious, you can leave baby powder out overnight and look for tracks in the morning, but it's not gonna help get rid of the little guys.

- Turds

Scientists call turds "droppings." Fresh turds are squishy and light brown, old turds are black and crusty. If you see a lot of turds, you have a lot of mice.

←TURD

- Weird Holes in the Wall

Not like the huge one your roommate left when he was blacked out drunk. These will be little beady holes, probably under the sink. Mice can chew through drywall no problem. If the gnaw mark is rough around the edges, it was probably made recently.

- Grease Marks

Mice are greasy. For some reason their fur is all oily, so when they rub up against things they leave dirty little smear marks. Sick!

- Little Puddles of Piss

Kind of looks like you spilled a drop of tea. Apparently you can use a UV light to spot pee puddles, but that seems like a lot of work.

- Inexplicable Stink

Could be dead mice rotting in your walls, could just be you.

## Keepin' it Humane

Look, the best way to make sure you don't get totally overrun is to store all your food really well. Get your

mom to send you some of her Tupperware and keep
all your munchies in it. Doritos on the counter are a
no-no. It's probably a good idea to keep your bread
in the fridge. Clean countertops and stovetops are
a must! If mice figure out they can stock up on the
crumbs your disgusting roommate refuses to clean
up, they're gonna throw a huge rager in your kitchen.

You can also try sealing up any mouse holes with

copper wire (get it at the hardware store). Some people say you can use steel wool, but steel wool rusts easily and eventually disintegrates. Mice can't chew through copper, so they'll chip a tooth and freak out and leave it alone. Aluminum foil might work, too.

## Pussy Power!

If you can swing it, get a cat! Cats are seriously your best bet for getting rid of mice. They are natural-born killers, so if you're trying to save lives this probably isn't the way to go. But it's the food chain, for Christ's sake. Get a grip.

Another cat option is to bring in the scrappiest, scariest looking street cat you can find and leave him in your apartment while you go to work. Your mouse will be dead by the time you get home, but your house will probably smell like cat pee and all your stuff will be all scratched up. Also you'll probably get fleas.

You know how cats sometimes leave dead animals on your doorstep or pillow? There are a few reasons why:

1.     He is giving you a tasty gift, like the equivalent of giving another human a meat and cheese platter. He loves you! He wants you to be well fed.

2.     He wants you to know what a serious and ferocious hunter he is. He is showing off his prowess and cunning. He wants you to know he is not to be messed with.

3.     He has noticed that you yourself are not such a great hunter and wants to show you how it's done.

It's gross, but you should reward Kitty with a small treat when he drags in his bloody spoils of war. Be thankful! He is looking out for you!

Maybe you hate cats, maybe you're allergic, or maybe you just don't want the hassle of having to care for another living thing. You can still use the pussy power to your advantage! Mice can smell cats from a mile away, so just put some kitty litter under your sink or wherever you think they're hanging out. They'll get all freaked out and won't come near it.

Catnip works the same way. Mice won't even mess

around with it. Catmint works, too. Added bonus: both contain this stuff called *nepeta*, which keeps away beetles, ants, and mosquitoes. You can buy nepeta oil, but it's pretty pricey (around thirty dollars a pop), and usually imported from somewhere exotic, like China or Oregon. You'll do just as well with straight up catnip. Any pet store will sell your average mid-grade nip, but you can get that hydroponic-grade herb from the hippies down at the farmers market. (Tip: hippies always grow the best shit.)

You can also just leave jars of cat pee all around your house. It'll smell terrible, but you won't have mice. Also, good luck collecting cat pee.

## Magic Potions

There's all kinds of new-age voodoo you can use to keep mice away. For starters, you can soak cotton balls in stuff they hate and then put them anywhere you think mice are getting in and out. Try using any of these oils:

Mice hate peppermint for some reason. Maybe because it smells fresh and clean. Make sure you use the real, legit, 100 percent pure oil and NOT the extract.

Free medical advice! Some people say peppermint oil helps with stubborn poops. People with IBS sometimes use it, and it's in some dietary supplements that claim to treat nausea, cramps, and morning sickness (effect on hangovers is unclear). We don't know about doses or anything, so do some research before you go guzzling it.

You can buy peppermint oil for less than ten bucks at Wal-Mart, and probably twice that at Whole Foods. If you want you can make a spray solution, just dilute the oil with a little bit of water.

Mice also hate lemon oil, lavender oil, and tea tree oil, so you can use them the same way. They all cost about the same (ten to fifteen dollars, depending on where you go).

You can also try eucalyptus oil. Use it like you would the peppermint oil, or smash up eucalyptus leaves and rub them all over everything. Use gloves, though, because if undiluted eucalyptus oil gets on your skin it'll make it all itchy and red and gross. Diabetics and pregnant chicks should also be careful with this stuff. Apparently eucalyptus oil messes with your blood sugar levels. Also, don't drink it (not even as a mixer). This stuff is fatal if ingested in high doses.

If you're doing the all-natural cotton ball thing, keep in mind that it can take awhile before you see results. And you gotta keep at it—change the cotton balls every day for a few weeks to a month, and if you're using sprays, spray every day. Maybe twice.

## MOTH BALLS

Moth balls might work. Leave them around like you would the cotton balls (any place you think mice are coming and going). This is maybe not the best option if you are the kind of person who is concerned about inhaling poisonous gases. Mothballs are just, like, pure insecticide, and apparently that vapor is toxic. Also they smell like stale old people.

DRIED SNAKE POOP

If you're a total badass, you can just leave a whole
bunch of dried snake poop around your house. Mice
hate snakes because snakes eat them whole, and
dried snake poop has no smell to humans, while
mice smell certain death. Apparently it keeps possums away, too. And of course you can buy it on the
internet: costs about fifteen bucks for five grams. If
you're cool enough to try this, write us and let us
know how it goes and we will induct you in to the
Rock 'N'Roll Extermination Hall of Fame.

# Catch-and-Release

Catch-and-release is kind of a dick move, because
the little dude is just gonna find someone else's
house to live in. Maybe if you live like the Unabomb-
er in the middle of nowhere you could pull it off, but
otherwise you might as well just hand the mouse off
to your next-door neighbor.

   If you insist on keeping the critter alive, there are

ways to effectively catch mice without killing them, but remember: unless you want them coming back you gotta release them AT LEAST two miles from your house. Any less than that and they can find their way back to you.

## THE PEANUT BUTTER FUN RUN

1.   Get a cardboard paper towel tube.

2.   Flatten one side of the tube so that it can balance on the edge of your counter or kitchen table. Leave a little more than half hanging off one side. If you need to, you can secure it with a little bit of tape, but it's gonna have to collapse so don't go crazy.

3.   Bait the end of the tube that's hanging off. Peanut butter works, or you can use any of the other good mouse baits found on page 35.

4.   Place an empty trash can underneath the baited edge that's hanging off. No trash bag! He'll be able to climb out if you use a trash bag. Also, the taller the trash can, the better.

It's supposed work like this: Mousey sees bait. Mousey runs through tube to get bait. (Mice are really into tubes and tunnels, so this is, like, double the fun for them.) Mousey reaches edge of tube and falls into the trash can. Then you have to collect him and figure out a way to secure him, get him into your car, and release him into the wild. Remember, go at least two miles! And wear gloves. Mice are gross.

If you can pull this one off, pat yourself on the back! Your mouse is some other sucker's problem now.

### THE COFFEE CAN HOLDING CELL

1.    Cut a two-inch hole in the lid of an empty coffee can. Folgers works, or Maxwell House.

2.    Throw in some disgusting smelling cheese, like bleu or gorgonzola. (See page 35 for the truth about mice and cheese. But you gotta use something real stinky for this one since they won't actually be able to *see* the bait. Plus, at the end of the day, they'll eat anything so just give it a shot.)

3.    Put the lid on.

4.    Make a ramp up the side of the coffee can. Use a butter knife or something. Maybe a spatula.

The mouse will squeeze his greasy little body through the hole in order to get to the cheese. Since the lid's on he won't be able to get out, and in the morning you'll have your very own prisoner of war.

## STORE-BOUGHT CATCH-AND-RELEASE TRAPS

Catch-and-release traps go for about twenty-five dollars. They come in one- and two-door varieties, but we have no idea what the difference is. Just throw some bait in one side and see what happens. These are for catching real animals like raccoons and skunks, and it seems like a total waste of time to set one up for a mouse. But whatever. It's your mouse.

# Catching Mice the Hardcore Way

## SNAP TRAPS

So, if you try all those pansy-ass tricks and still have mouse turds all over the place, it's time get serious. Go into any store ever and buy a few of those classic wooden snap traps. They're pretty cheap, but don't be stingy and get the cheapest ones you can find. You'll catch more mice with a sturdy, solid trap than a flimsy one. Get a few. You're gonna set more than one, and chances are you're gonna need them in the future. If you had mice once, you're probably going to have them again, especially if you ignore our ad-

vice about storing food the right way (see page 24).

Snap traps are probably the best way to get rid of mice (besides cats), but you can't just wander blindly into battle. You have to know what you're doing. There's a strategy here, people! Start with luring them in.

## SOME FOODS THAT MAKE GOOD MOUSE BAIT

peanut butter

cookies

dried fruit

nuts

cooked bacon

bacon grease

raw meat

oatmeal

fresh bread

cake

donuts

sardines

chocolate

olives

candies (Skittles, Dots, Jujubcs, gumdrops)

The idea that mice really like cheese is a myth, probably started by some cartoon somewhere. They'll eat it (they'll eat anything), but it's probably not the best bait.

So, hopefully by now you have some idea where your mice are coming from. If you don't, start looking for holes. A lot of times it's under the sink. Also remember that they're looking for food, so put some traps around trash cans, recycle bins, compost piles, or secret food hoards. Other primo spots are behind ovens, stoves, and refrigerators. They like dark, dingy lairs, and they like narrow tunnels, like the space between your fridge and your counter.

Three or four traps should do it. Put them along the walls, parallel to the baseboards, with the bait hook facing the wall. Mice don't really like hanging out in the middle of rooms. It makes them feel vulnerable and exposed, so they stick to corners and floorboards.

Some things to know when setting your traps:

- Don't go all crazy handling the traps. Mice will get suspicious if your scent is all over the place. Might be a good idea to wear gloves.
- Get rid of all other food sources except for the bait. If you starve the little fuckers out,

they'll be forced to eat the Jujube you left on the trap.

• Don't use TOO much bait. Mice have teeny little brains, but they are still smart enough to figure out how to eat bait from a trap without setting it off. If they can easily reach the bait from a safe distance, they'll take it back to their friends and have a feast and you'll look like a total sucker. To avoid this, glue the bait down.

• Don't set the traps for the first few nights. This is important. Put a different kind of bait on each trap (see page 35) and wait. This is like an all-you-can-eat buffet for mice, and like true Americans they'll get all fat and greedy and keep making multiple trips. You want them to get really comfortable eating off the traps. After two or three nights, set them all the traps. D-Day.

If you don't see results in three days, move the traps and switch the bait. Patience is a virtue.

Hopefully this goes without saying, but always clean up any

blood and guts, and never reuse traps. Also, touching dead mice is gross. Don't do it. Get some rubber gloves and throw that sucker in a plastic bag, then put it in the trash outside. Nobody wants a dead mouse in their kitchen trash.

## GLUE TRAPS

Glue traps are total bullshit. They don't cause sudden death, so many people feel that they are a more humane option than snap traps. But once a mouse gets caught in a glue trap his fur gets all tangled up, and he starts freaking out so much that his skin rips off. We know people who have found little clumps of bloody hair in the traps, but no mouse. (One lady woke up to find one little bloody leg in her glue trap!) If you do manage to catch one with a glue trap, it's up to you to put him out of his misery. You could step

Rodents can't burp or fart, so any carbonated beverage will make their little stomachs explode. If you're into it, leave out some Orange Crush or some beer, but be careful: roaches love both.

on him, or drop a book on him, or smother him to death. The idea that you can release him back into the wild is ludicrous. Good luck getting him off the trap in one piece. Plus he's probably all traumatized from the time he spent as your sticky prisoner of war. We say don't waste your time.

## DIY MOUSE POISONS

You could also cook up some homemade poisons. Ingredients are cheap, but be warned: if one of those little dudes dies in your wall, it's gonna smell terrible. Put the poison in places you suspect mice might be hanging out: under the sink, around the trash can, and in dark corners like the ones behind your refrigerator or stove.

These two recipes will seem like a delicious treat to the mouse. Little do they know it will be their last.

- 1 part flour
- 1 part icing
- 1 part portland cement (about ten bucks at the hardware store)

Mix it all up and leave it out overnight. Hopefully they're into it. They won't be into digesting cement, so with any luck you'll never see that mouse again.

You can also try:
- dry cement powder
- cornflower

Mix 50/50 in a small, shallow dish. Apparently the cement powder makes them really thirsty, and once they get a drink of water their stomachs turn to cement.

DROWNIN' MICE

We've only heard of these being used in farmhouses and barns, but we guess you could set either up in your kitchen if you wanted. Both are designed for taking out multiple mice at a time, so they could come in handy if you're battling an army.

1. Get a giant bucket and fill it with water.

2. Put a whole bunch of peanut butter around the rim.

3. Get some 2 x 4s and prop 'em against the

side of the bucket like ramps.

It's like a pool party, except mice can't swim.


For an advanced variation, try this one.

You'll need:

- something sharp and stabby, like an awl or a screwdriver or a knife
- a beer can (or a pop can, if you're sober)
- a wire hanger
- a mop bucket
- a 2 x 4
- peanut butter and a knife (for spreading!)

1.    Punch a hole through the bottom of the empty beer can. (You can start with a full beer and shotgun it until it's empty. Works just as well.)

2.    Uncurl the wire hanger so that it's in sort of a straight line.

3.    Thread the wire through both holes of the beer can.

4.    Cover the outside of the beer can with pea-nut butter.

5.     Fill the bucket with water. Rest both ends of the wire hanger on either side of the bucket so that the can is in the middle, hanging over the water.

6.     Use the 2 x 4 to make a ramp.

It's like the log roll in the strong man competition! Except mice can't swim.

# CHAPTER TWO:
# COCKROACHES

Everyone's heard that cockroaches will inherit the earth. People often assume that roaches will be the last species alive after the apocalypse, that they can survive nuclear war, subzero temperatures, and decapitation. These are only half-truths. They're survivors, for sure, but they're not indestructible. In this chapter we'll teach you how to wipe out these freaks on the cheap.

# Roach Biology

Cockroaches live everywhere. They can easily adapt to almost any environment, but they prefer warm weather (like the kind in your apartment). Some species are able to live without food or water for more than a month, and some can go without air for forty-five minutes. One study found that cockroaches could bounce back after being underwater for a half hour. Despite their superhero-like capabilities for survival, the life span of your average cockroach is only about three or four months. (Exotic species like the Madagascar hissing cockroach can live for up to two years.)

Part of the reason cockroaches are so damn resilient is because they have a complicated network of breathing tubes called *tracheae*. This helps them survive in conditions most insects could not. The tracheae are not attached to their heads, so they breathe through their skeletons and do not depend on windpipes or lungs. They actually don't have lungs at all.

Some larger species will force air in and out of their breathing holes (called *spiracles*). This could be considered breathing, but is not really breathing as we know it.

## Love Lives

Cockroaches are all about pheromones. They emit scents that tell other cockroaches where to find food and water, as well as the rest of their cockroach posse. These scents are extra important when it comes time to find someone to bone. The female cockroach emits a smell into the air to let the males know that she is ready to get it on. Picture this: a female cockroach atop your kitchen counter, wings spread out as wide as they will go. She stands tall and emits her love potion number nine, then sits and waits for her prince charming to come along and whisk her away to paradise. Or she lets the first guy who shows up have a go. Prince charming or not, he will provide her with tons of sperm, which she'll store away and use to fertilize her next few batches of eggs. This means she'll go her whole life without ever mating again, unlike rats, who can't stop getting it on with anyone and everyone.

## Social Lives

Cockroaches practice something called *group-based decision-making*. This means they make choices as a collective rather than as individuals. An example: A group of scientists offered fifty cockroaches a choice of three different shelters. The scientists made each of these shelters really comfy and cozy. Although each shelter could have easily housed more than fifty cockroaches each, all fifty cockroaches swarmed into one shelter. Group instinct told them that sticking together would make it easier to pick up chicks, find food, and keep warm (remember: cockroaches are really into being warm).

Even though they ride together, die together, cockroaches do not form hierarchies. Their decisions are mutual, and every member of the swarm is in agreement. Sort of like a cult, except there's no leader telling everyone else what to do. Somehow they just know what's best for their homies. (This doesn't mean it's always smooth sailing. Males tend to get a little competitive when it comes to females. They've been known to battle each other for first dibs on a super hot babe.)

Cockroaches can recognize members of their own families, and they prefer to live with their parents and grandparents. They can tell who's who by the chemical trails left in their poop. Cockroaches are so needy that they'll often get weak or sick when they're left alone. If they spend lots of time alone as babies they'll take longer to grow into adults, and they'll also have trouble finding a place in the herd (as well as a mate) later in life.

This cockroach camaraderie does not extend to feeding time, however. Hungry cockroaches have been known to tear off each others' limbs, even fight to the death for a scrap of food. After all, what sort of evolutionary significance would come from letting your neighbors eat all your food?

Cockroaches are nocturnal creatures, doing their business in the nighttime after you go to sleep. That's why you always (well, hopefully not *always*) see them when you open your refrigerator for a late-night snack. The light freaks them out, but they love dark corners and crevices. If you do happen to see one during the daylight, you've probably got quite a population on your hands. A daylight cockroach is probably the weak little runt of the herd. He has to come out and look for food during daytime hours because he doesn't have what it takes to compete with the big dogs.

So, what about the theory that they will survive the apocalypse? Cockroaches can survive about fifteen times more radiation than humans can, but they're not *totally* resistant. Radiation affects cells when they are dividing, and a cockroach's cells divide only when they are molting, or shedding their skin. Cockroaches molt only a few times during their lifespan, and never during adulthood. So, during nuclear fallout, only the cockroaches who are molting would be affected, but human cells divide constantly, so it would wipe us out. Fruit flies actually have a much higher chance than cockroaches of surviving nuclear war (their cells never divide).

## Role as Pests

A good cockroach prevention strategy is to seal any points of entry. (Actually, that is a good prevention strategy for every pest in this book.) You should know that cockroaches are fond of right angles—they have a tendency to set up shop in areas where the wall meets the floor, a cabinet meets the wall, the countertop rests on the cabinet, and especially around the baseboards. If you've got huge gaps in these areas, caulk it up! Silicone caulk works best, and it's not a bad idea to put some roach gel in the crack first. That stuff goes for around ten to fifteen bucks at the hardware store, but we're guessing you can probably find some cheaper generic-brand stuff at the dollar store.

Like rodents, cockroaches can pass around disgusting microbes that can be harmful to humans. They also have chemicals in their poop that can aggravate asthma symptoms and possibly cause breathing troubles in more feeble humans, like children and old people. But as far as deadly diseases go, that's about as bad as it gets when it comes to cockroaches. Nobody's ever died from one before.

Just because you have cockroaches in your house doesn't mean you're dirty or gross. They'll set up shop anywhere there is food to eat, which could be a clean kitchen just as easily as a dirty one. The best way make sure you don't get totally overrun is to keep your food stored right. Tupperware is your friend. Use it to store flour, rice, quinoa, basically anything wheat- or flour-based. (Flour is the cockroach's carbohydrate of choice.)

Cockroaches can survive longer without food than they can without water, so try not to leave dishes soaking in the sink. Even if your kitchen is totally crumb-free, those little bastards will swarm on a puddle of water like it's a goddamn desert oasis.

And now, here's a poem:

Dishwashing tonight at il Fiasco
ritzy Italian restaurant
on Commercial Street
A five-top family was seated
had already ordered
when a teenage son
found inside an ice cube
in the cola
he was drinking
a frozen cockroach
A cockroach!
Frozen!
He was so grossed out that he couldn't eat
neither could his teenage brother
equally sickened
so us rats back in the kitchen
ate their steak
ate their lamb shank
ate their halibut
post-apocalyptic
The old cockroach
in an ice cube trick
cheap imitation of a fly in amber
from our dinosaur days

—Jeff Jewell, Alaska

# Waging War

There are tons of ways to get rid of roaches without using chemicals. There are two solutions in particular that do the trick: boric acid and diatomaceous earth.

## MEDITATIONS ON BORIC ACID

Boric acid is probably your best all-natural bet for killing cockroaches. (Ants, too, but more on that later.) It's cheap and easy to find: a bottle of it in powdered form should cost you less than five bucks, and you can get it at any hardware store. We've seen it at dollar stores, and also at that one store called the internet. It's sort of poisonous, so before you go sprinkling it all over your house there are a few things you should know.

Boric acid is *almost* all natural. It's like a mineral or something. Some German guy was the first dude to prepare it, but the Greeks were using it way back in the day to clean and preserve foods. When it gets on bugs, it slowly melts their exoskeletons, so you won't get instant results. But don't worry: it spreads around really easily, so know that they're going back to their colonies and getting it all over their cockroach brethren. Use gloves when you're handling it, and DON'T GET IT WET! Boric acid loses its effectiveness when it gets wet, like a gremlin.*

**Listen up, y'all: boric acid is poisonious if eaten or inhaled in large quantities.** We're telling you this now so you don't come for us when your roommate snorts it all. We should also tell you that long-term exposure has been linked to kidney problems. Oh, and it once shrunk some dogs' balls in a lab study. Kind of goes without saying that children are more susceptible to the dangers of boric acid, so keep it out of reach of the little brats. **If you have kids in your house and you are using boric acid:** make sure it's in small doses and out of their reach.

*Editor's note: You can use borax instead of boric acid. Borax is an old-timey laundry detergent and hand soap. Apparently it will also whiten your teeth. Either will do the job, but we recommend pure boric acid because it's stronger, and it's usually cheaper.

Look, as long as you don't eat it, snort it, or bathe in it you're gonna be okay. When used correctly, boric acid is actually really useful. Just look at all the things it can do!

• It's an antiseptic! Seriously, this stuff gets used in all sorts of cures, from minor scrapes and burns to vaginal douches! Most of those emergency eyewash stations you always saw in shop class have a very, very small amount of boric acid in them. It can also prevent athlete's foot.

• It preserves stuff! Mostly wood. In certain mixtures it keeps wood from rotting. It also cures cattle hides, calfskins, and sheepskins.

• It's lube! (Not that kind, though.) But in case you want to lube up ceramic or metal surfaces, it can do that when dissolved in vegetable oil.

• It's used in nuclear power! Somehow. We don't get it because it's really complicated. Something about slowing down fission and neutrons and stuff.

• It's sooooo industrious! Used in fiberglass, jewelry, LCD panels, and Silly Putty!!

•     It's used in pyrotechnics! Fireworks are so sweet!

So you see?! It might shrink your testes, but would YOU want to live in a world without Silly Putty?!

## IT'S PRONOUNCED DIE-OH-TOM-A-SHUSS EARTH

Food-grade *diatomaceous earth* is a nontoxic soft rock that comes ground up into a fine powder. You can get it at the hardware store for about ten to fifteen dollars. When insects come into contact with diatomaceous earth, their little bodies get all cut up and all their fluids leak out. Then they die from dehydration. (Oh, the humanity!)

# Recipes for Disaster

The good thing about roaches is it's easy to do some damage because of their cultish group mentality. Where one roach eats, others definitely eat. One visit to the poison buffet could mean certain death for a whole family.

1.    Mix equal parts cocoa powder (be warned:

that shit stains) and flour with diatomaceous earth. Sprinkle this magic mixture anywhere you suspect roach activity. The cocoa powder attracts them, the DE snuffs 'em out.

2.    One part boric acid, one part flour.

3.    One part molasses, one part boric acid. This is a sticky one! We know a guy who used it on the ceiling since he couldn't put powder up there. It worked, and he no longer felt uncomfortable having babes over.

4.    If you prefer a sticky paste mixture to a powdery one, you could also try this slightly more complicated variation. You'll need:

- boric acid
- maple syrup
- flour

Flush any dead roaches you find immediately. They can come back to life!!! (Actually, they're not really dead. They're just lying dormant.) Also roaches are known to have cannibalistic tendencies. They'll feed on the corpses of their loved ones if they have to, so dead roaches could attract more roaches.

- a popsicle stick
- a mixing bowl

Mix together two parts boric acid, one part flour, and enough syrup to get the mixture to a peanut-butter-like consistency. Then smear, smear, smear!

If hand-to-hand combat is your thing, put some soap and water into a spray bottle and spray the hell out of any cockroach you see. Remember that cockroaches breathe through their skeletons? The soap chokes them out. We like this method because it's clean and won't require any cleaning up (except for the dead roach, anyway).

# Jar Traps!

If you're into crafts, you could make a jar trap. They're cheap and easy, and they do the job. If you're using jar traps and finding tons of roaches on the regular, chances are you've got a serious infestation going. Step up your boric acid game and sprinkle it around the bases of the jars.

These DIY cockroach traps will catch your prey

alive, in case you want to torture or study them later:

• Get an old coffee can. Put some coffee grounds and a little bit of water in the bottom, enough so the mixture is soupy, but not a total swimming pool. Lean the jar up against the wall at an angle so whatever crawls in can't crawl out. Change the grounds every couple of days. (Not a coffee drinker? A banana peel will work, too.) If you find any roaches alive, throw the can in the freezer overnight. Roaches can't survive the subzero temperatures. They'll die in there.

> Roaches love to party! Beer is a very, very good roach bait, so make sure to rinse out your empties before you throw them out.

• Another homemade trap can be made using Vaseline and an empty glass jar. An old pasta jar, pickle jar, or even baby food jar will work. Wrap the outside of the glass jar with a piece of paper, because roaches can't climb up glass. You could put some bait in there, some dried up pasta or a crumb or something. Smear Vaseline along the inside rim of the jar.

Roaches will be able to get inside the jar, but they can't climb through Vaseline, so they won't be able to get out. If to your horror you find any roaches in there alive, pour in a mixture of hot water and liquid soap. That should do it.

• You can also use a two-liter bottle. Cut off the top, curved part of the bottle. Invert it so that the nozzle is inside the body of the two-liter like a little funnel. Tape those two parts together. Pour some beer down the funnel. They'll crawl down to get a sip of the sweet nectar, but they won't be able to get out so they'll drown in there. (There are worse ways to go.)

• If you're a foodie, you could always try:
    1 clove garlic
    1 small onion
    1 tbsp cayenne pepper
    1 qt hot water

Soak all the ingredients in the hot water for one hour, and then stir. (You don't need to chop anything up. Just throw it in.)

Leave the pot on the countertop or on the floor overnight. When roaches eat cayenne pepper, it makes their heads explode like in *Scanners*. (We're kidding! We don't know how it works. It just does.) Maybe keep this one out of reach of pets? Doesn't seem like it'd kill them, but it can't be pleasant for them, either.

### Real-Life Roach Nightmares

"I used to live in Charleston, South Carolina. The cockroaches down there (they call them palmetto bugs) are really huge and disgusting AND THEY FLY. I rented this weird little room off the back of somebody's house. It was more like a garage, really, but it was cheap so I figured, whatever. The first night I was there I kept hearing noises. I turned on the light and watched at least 100 of those little fuckers scurry into the cracks in the walls. One flipped out and started flying around all frantically. I didn't know what to do so I just sat there weeping. I had to sleep with my lights on as long as I lived there. If I turned them off I'd hear them come crawling back. It was an absolute nightmare."

—DA, Brooklyn

# CHAPTER THREE:
## RATS

If you have rats in your home, God help you. Mice are gross, but they are a fairly common nuisance and are usually pretty easy to control once you put your mind to it. Rats are a different story. They play hard ball.

Rats are very hard to get rid of. They have out-lasted wars, disease, and radiation fallout, and if they can survive nuclear testing, they can survive in your apartment.

Don't worry. It's not totally hopeless. There are some ways to get rid of them once they've taken up residence, but before we get there we should look at why they're such good enemies.

## Origin of the Species

Rats have been around for a very, very long time. Their origins trace back to Asia, and today there are many different species wreaking havoc all across the globe. The Norway rat (also known as the brown rat) is the most common. This is the city rat—the one you see in sewers and trash cans. Black rats (also called roof rats) are more common in the southern states and on the West Coast.

Don't be confused by the name: Norway rats probably originated from Asia. They started spreading to other parts of the world sometime in the Middle Ages, arriving on the East Coast of the United States by the late eighteenth century. They now live almost everywhere humans do, and like mice, rats are commensal. This means they benefit from our existence without giving anything back in return, like a spoiled child or an ex-boyfriend.

The reason rats are so difficult to get rid of is twofold: they are very smart, and they are tremendous breeders.

# Love Lives

It's been said that there are as many rats in the world as there are humans, but this is probably false. In reality, it's almost impossible to know exactly how many rats there are because of how quickly they multiply. Let's look at the numbers.

Female rats give birth about three to five times a year, in litters from five to twenty-two (seven seems to be the lucky number). They can get pregnant just eighteen hours after giving birth.

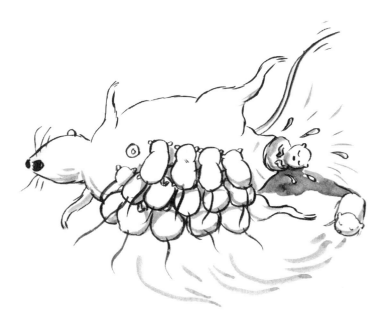

Rats have sex for pleasure. Weaker male rats who have been exiled from their colony will form all-male rat colonies and have sex with each other.

Rats have sex about twenty times a day (not even porn stars get that much action). Not unlike human males, male rats will have sex with as many female rats as possible—some studies suggest this can mean up to twenty females in six hours.

One pair of rats has the potential to produce fifteen thousand descendants per year, which is just totally fucking crazy.

When rats are killed off (by humans, other rats, or natural causes), the pregnancy rates among the surviving rats double. When one dies, another takes its place, and the surviving rats get bigger, fatter, and more intimidating.

## Sewer Smarts

Rats are much smarter than house mice. They possess something called *metacognition*, a Latin term which roughly translates to "knowing about knowing." Only three types of animals are known to have metacognition: humans, some primates, and rats. Rats possess brain functions that allow problem-solving, learning, memory and memorization, and reasoning. Like a college student taking a test, a rat knows what it knows, and what it doesn't know.*

But rats aren't all book smarts. They've got street smarts, too, which probably better explains why they've lasted so goddamn long. They have all kinds of superpowers.

RATS CAN:

- swim for more than a half mile
- tread water for THREE DAYS
- gnaw through concrete and lead
- collapse their skeletons and fit through a hole no bigger than a quarter
- go for two weeks without sleeping (this means NONSTOP EATING)

*Editor's note: Lab rats and city rats are the same species, so the rat being taught to memorize tunnels is not so different from the rat crawling around in your garbage late at night. While lab rats are more refined than their scrappy, sewer-dwelling cousins (the result of careful, controlled breeding), it's safe to assume they possess the same brain functions and capabilities.

- survive atomic-bomb testing
- memorize
- communicate
- plan ahead and execute plans
- go one to two weeks without water
- fall five stories without injury
- jump three feet in the air from a flat surface
- leap four feet horizontally
- detect poison in incredibly small increments
- speak Spanish (not really)

They've obviously honed their survival skills and figured out how to adapt to almost every environment. They would make the ultimate Survivor contestant.

## NUCLEAR BLAST? WHAT NUCLEAR BLAST?

The United States tested nuclear weapons in the Marshall Islands about forty times between the years 1946 and 1958. Although not much is known about rat population on the islands before the tests, it's largely believed that at least one species of rat was able to withstand the blasts. The rats probably survived by burrowing really far down into the ground. Now, more than thirty years later, the rodent population of the Marshall Islands exhibits almost no side effects from the radiation, which suggests they have adapted freakishly well.

## Social Lives and Personal Hygiene

Rats are hierarchal creatures. Even rats living in pairs will have a dominant rat, or "alpha rat." In larger groups (which are much more common than pairs), the alpha rat will appoint a second in command, a lieutenant he can boss around and send out into the world to do his bidding. The moods and interactions of these two rats will determine the vibes among the other rats living in that colony. In other words: when alpha ain't happy, ain't nobody happy.

Understanding rats means understanding their environment, which, inconveniently enough, is our environment. Humans and rats live, literally, side by side. City rats live in elaborately constructed underground burrows, with a series of tunnels leading to den-like common areas where they store food and have sex. Rats pad their dens with luxurious materials like shredded plastic bags, wood chips (these are, ironically, often gnawed from the wooden traps that humans use to kill them), or grass. The entrances to their underground lairs are small and inconspicuous. They will often dig a "bolt hole," which is an emergency exit at the back of their burrow, used for a quick escape if necessary. They camouflage their bolt hole by covering it with dirt and trash. They

Year of the Rat!
According to the Chinese zodiac, those born in the year of the rat possess wit, imagination, and curiosity. They are good observers with strong intuition. They are energetic and charming, while perhaps having a tendency to become a bit aggressive at times. They are very social and give good advice. It is not known whether or not brown rats possess any of these characteristics.

often build burrows under apartment buildings, restaurants, or subway stations—basically anywhere with easy access to food scraps. (Rats rarely stray too far from their burrows, so location is key.)

Humans have adopted an "us vs. them" mentality when it comes to rats, which is not hard to understand given their army-like numbers and terrifying capabilities for spreading disease and destruction. Their bad reputations are a result of their jarring psychical characteristics (those disgusting naked tails!) and poor hygiene. They are, admittedly, not the cleanest of creatures.

Rats are greasy like their mice cousins (runs in the family). Their fur contains lanolin, a lotion-like substance that lets them slip through holes easily. Exterminators looking for rat colonies will look for rub marks along walls and alleyways. Rats like to be constantly touching walls because this helps them memorize routes. Exterminators will follow the greasy trail to find burrows or colonies.

Admittedly, they are not ideal neighbors. But it's

important to understand that we share a space with them, like it or not. They've been here as long as humans have, and they are fierce competitors in the turf war. Their sheer numbers are a good indication of who *really* owns the city.

# Diseases!

Rats carry diseases we know about, and diseases we don't know about (yet). If you get bitten by a rat, wash it IMMEDIATELY (duh), and call a doctor if it starts to look nasty. These are some of our favorite rat diseases, but it's definitely not a complete list.

## TYPHUS!

There are lots of different kinds of typhus. The kind that rat fleas carry is called *murine typhus* or *endemic typhus*. Symptoms include headache, fever, muscle pain, joint pain, nausea, and puking everywhere. If you get murine typhus you might develop a rash, and you might experience confusion, stupor, seizures, or have trouble balancing.

### Real-Life Rat Nightmares

"So my friend knew this dude who had rats real bad. He said he set out snap traps, but the rats never took the bait.

Instead of calling an exterminator, he just put up one of those baby gate things in his kitchen to keep them out of the rest of the house. That obvoiusly didn't work, and the rats just started taking over his whole place. It got so bad that his roommate moved out and left him to deal with it. Eventually the rats started running around his bedroom at night, so what did this guy do? He just kept building his bed higher and higher so that they wouldn't crawl on him at night. But like, did he think rats couldn't climb stuff? It's the stupidest idea I've ever heard. I wonder where he is now. Probably in the hospital with some disgusting disease."

—ZS, Queens

Don't worry! Endemic typhus can be treated with antibiotics unless you're really old, severely disabled, or have a weakened immune system. In that case, there's no hope for you and you'll probably die a slow painful death. (We're kidding! You can probably still bounce back.)

## THE BUBONIC PLAGUE!

Everyone's favorite rat disease. What we know to be the bubonic plague is caused by a bacteria called *Y. pestis*. Known nowadays as the Black Death, it killed an estimated seventy-five to two hundred million people in fourteenth century Europe, which was about 30 to 60 percent of the population at the time (that's crazy!). It originated in China and spread to Europe by the Silk Road, a historical network of trade routes. There have been a few different outbreaks throughout history, including almost one thousand cases reported in the twentieth century. These days it can be cured with antibiotics, but you have to catch it early and start treatment within the first twenty-four hours of symptoms. (In the Middle

Ages, doctors believed that bad smells would cure the plague. They used human poop and pee to treat patients, which of course just made it worse. Other "cures" included thinking happy thoughts, drinking good wine, and avoiding fruits.)

### How to Tell if You Have the Plague

Symptoms of the plague usually show up two to five days after exposure. The first signs are swollen lymph glands, which are tiny little oval-shaped organs that you have all throughout your body. After they swell up you'll develop little pustules called *buboes* in the armpits, groin, and neck. Then you'll probably get gangrene in your fingers, toes, nose, or lips. Of course you'll have your general flu-like symptoms (chills, fever, muscle cramps), and you'll also vomit blood! Your whole body will ache, probably because your skin is literally rotting off your body while you are still alive. If you experience any of these symptoms, call your doctor and say a prayer.

## RAT-BITE FEVER!

Rat-bite fever is most common in Japan, but cases have been reported in the United States, Europe, Australia, and Africa. It's transmitted through rodent secretions like mucus, spit, poop, or pee. Weasels, gerbils, and squirrels can also carry rat-bite fever, and dogs and cats that have been infected are capable of infecting humans. Rat-bite fever is often indicated by redness or inflammation around the infected area (probably a bite), and symptoms include chills, fever, vomiting, headaches, and muscle aches. Sometimes your joints will swell up and hurt really bad, and ulcers may develop on the hands and feet.

## LEPTOSPIROSIS!

Leptospirosis is transmitted through water that has been contaminated by toxic animal pee. Rats and moles are the most common carriers, but dogs, deer, rabbits, cows, sheep, possums, and skunks can carry it, too. It has a wide range of symptoms, and sometimes people with Leptospirosis show no symptoms at all. Those who do exhibit symptoms have reported flu-like symptoms (fever, chills, vomiting, severe headache), as well as jaundice, red eyes, diarrhea, and a rash. Severe cases can lead to meningitis, hearing loss, and liver failure.

## Appetite for Destruction

No other mammal besides man causes as much death or economic devastation as rats. It's been estimated that in the past century alone rats have caused more than ten million human deaths (remember: this is post-plague we're talking about). Rats and other rodents can eat or spoil up to one-fifth of the world's food supply. We don't just mean by crawling all over produce at farmers markets and fruit stands. We mean mass destruction on a global scale.

Bamboo blooms every fifty years in southeastern Bangladesh. Rats love bamboo seeds, so when it starts to sprout they go nuts and swarm the rural villages. Once they've wiped out all the bamboo, they move on to other plants like rice, ginger, turmeric, and chili. They can destroy entire fields of crops, which causes shortages in the villages and

> Dog poop is a rat attractant! Just one more reason to pick up after your dog, and to bitch out your neighbors for not doing so.

abroad (these crops are important exports for Bangladesh). The situation got so bad that the country sponsored a rat-killing contest, destroying about 25 million rats in a year. (The winner killed about forty thousand singlehandedly. His prize? A measly fourteen-inch color TV. It wasn't even a flatscreen.)

For another good example of just how much damage rats can cause, we turn to The Island Formerly Known as Rat Island, Alaska. Sometime around 1780, a Japanese ship wrecked off the Alaskan coast. Rats are very good swimmers, and a whole bunch of them swam their way to safety in the freezing cold Alaskan waters (which, unfortunately, was more than the sailors could manage). The rats quickly destroyed wildlife populations on the island, particularly among the native seabirds who had no natural defenses against the rodent invaders. In 2007, the US Fish and Wildlife Service began testing eradication methods, needing a solution that would not wipe out other species living on the island. They spent a week and a half dumping poison onto the island. Afterwards, they found no signs of living rats, but plenty of signs of birds nesting. They declared the operation a success, and in 2012 Rat Island was officially renamed Hawadax Island.

Rats are nocturnal creatures. If you see one in the daytime, chances are it's the runt of the colony—forced to look for food and mates in the daytime when the more dominant rats aren't around to compete with. Don't worry: a daytime rat is probably not rabid. Rodents are almost never infected with rabies. In fact, no rodent has ever transmitted rabies to a human in the United States.

## Sorry, PETA

Because of their high levels of brain activity

(and because they breed so easily), rats are a favorite in lab testing. This scientific testing helps scientists better understand all kinds of important stuff like genetics, brain activity, and the effects of drugs.

Scientists have recently transmitted brain waves between two rats using the internet. Don't ask us about specifics, but we can tell you that it goes like this:

Scientists train Rat #1 to press a lever whenever he sees a little red light. If Rat #1 does this correctly, he gets rewarded with a drink of water.

Then, using an internet connection, scientists transmit this brain activity to Rat #2, who's isolated in a separate compartment, and therefore hasn't learned that "level = reward."

But after they plant Rat #1's brain waves in him, Rat #2 knows to press the lever to get a reward. He does this correctly over 70 percent of the time. That's crazy! Maybe one day they'll use this trick on humans and we'll all be geniuses.

# Catchin' Rats

If you're looking for ways to keep rats away without killing them, good luck. Let us know if you find anything. Kidding! There are a few things you can try.

Like with mice, the best prevention is to KEEP YOUR SHIT CLEAN. Keep a lid on your trash, store leftovers in airtight containers, and make sure your space is regularly swept, mopped, and disinfected. Rats are looking for food, and if you've got any around they will scavenge and pillage. If you live in an apartment building, bug the hell out of your super until your building's trash is properly stored. He should also be hiring exterminators and placing poison around the outside of your building. (But everyone knows that this is not always the case. Most of us haven't even met our supers.)

## SONIC REPELLERS

These deliver high-frequency sounds that humans and pets can't hear. If you wanna get really serious, there are some that deliver electromagnetic waves through the wiring in your house. Prices vary from about ten to fifty dollars, and we can't guarantee their effectiveness. (Reviews vary.)

It's true that rats can get into your residence through the sewer pipes. To keep them from crawling in through your kitchen sink, pour one cup of bleach down the drain every month. You can also mix one cup of baking soda and one cup of vinegar for the same effect. Afterward, rinse with boiling water.

Rats have been known to magically appear in toilet

Rat meat is considered a delicacy in certain parts of India, and here in New York we can't stand to be behind the food trends. One artist hosted a $100-a-plate dinner that claimed to explore "post-apocalyptic themes of urban survival." The main course: a rat and goat cheese crostini. But dinner-goers were outraged to learn that the rat meat was not locally sourced, imported instead from a "clean and safe facility" on the West Coast. (Hey, it's New York! We prefer to eat our own.)

### Real-Life Rat Nightmares

"Once I was coming home from the bar really late at night. Or early in the morning, whatever. I was one-eyeing it on the train ride home (should have taken a cab, but hey) and trying not to fall asleep when I noticed a few of the other passengers scuffling around. Some Japanese tourists were crouched on the seats taking pictures of something, and that's when I noticed a rat climbing all over this sleeping guy! He had an open bag of Andy Capp Hot Fries resting on his gut, and the rat was just straight up grabbing fries from the bag and eating them like a snack. This went on for a few stops. Nobody woke the guy up. I had to get off a few stops later and that rat was still going strong when I did. Freaked me out, man. Now I never eat on the train, and I sure as hell don't sleep, either."

—JM, Manhattan

bowls. This is not a myth. Keep the lid closed, and if you do find one in your toilet, flush it! But squirt some dishwashing liquid in first. This gets rid of all those disgusting oils on their fur, and without those oils they can't stay afloat.

# Methods for Total Eradication

Honestly, if you've got rats, we recommend calling in the pros. But if you're as poor as we are, this isn't really an option. Fear not—there are some things you can do on your own, without an exterminator or a witch doctor.

### TRAPPIN' RATS

It's harder to catch a rat with a snap trap than it is a mouse. Rats are smarter than mice, and they'll know if you're trying to punk them. If you think you have what it takes to snag one the old-fashioned way, make sure you buy those jumbo snap traps that are specifically made for rats. You should definitely set out more than one. We recommend taping rat traps to the floor, because rats have been known to drag away the wooden traps, shred them, and use the gnawed up wood to pad their little rat dens.

We definitely recommend using gloves when baiting rat traps. Or, at the very least, wash your hands

before AND after. Mice are dumb and might ignore your human scent if they think they'll be able to eat, but rats are very suspicious and not easily fooled.

You can probably trap a rat with just about any bait (especially any from the list of mouse bait on page 35), but exterminators say peanut butter, bread soaked in bacon grease, apples, potatoes, raw bacon, and raisins have all been known to get results. One exterminator said pecans will get them every time, and one rat owner said peas are your best bet.

Just like with mouse traps, bait the traps for a few nights in a row, but do not set them. Rats are keen observers of their surroundings, and it takes a while for them to get comfortable with any new objects in their environment. Rats come out at night, so set your traps in the evening and check them in the morning. If the bait is gone, you've probably got company. Or a really hungry roommate. After two or three nights of baiting the traps, set them and say a prayer.

SOME THINGS TO KNOW IF YOU ARE TRYING TO
TRAP RATS WITH A SNAP TRAP:

1.    It will take longer to get a rat in a trap than a mouse. Be patient. In the meantime, try to forget about them crawling around in your pipes and walls.

2.    Rats who live in colonies will send out feeble, weak rats to investigate new situations, like a suspicious-looking wooden block with a nugget of cheese on it. (As mentioned on page 70, sometimes the alpha will send the second-in-command.) Any change in their environment will arouse suspicion, which is why it's important to bait the traps for multiple nights in a row before you set them.

3.    If you do happen to catch a rat in a trap, congratulations!    While wearing gloves, put the dead rat AND THE TRAP into a plastic bag, and throw it into a tight-

New York Rat Moment!

The owner of a BMW once found some rat droppings in her car. She retreated to the house, where she then called the exterminator to come out and open her car door for her.

The rat was gone.

ly sealed garbage container. WASH YOUR HANDS. Now wash them again. Now sanitize. Once you catch a rat with a trap, you will not be able to catch another one with that same trap. They will smell rat on any reused trap and they will not be fooled into the same fate. But who would reuse a trap, honestly.

4.    If you're getting good results, keep on trappin' away. Use whatever bait works for you. But don't put the traps in the same places over and over. Rats are creatures of habit and often take the same routes to and from food sources, so it's important to switch up locations. Once one of their buddies dies in that trap in the far corner of the sink, they'll know what's up. They won't subject themselves to the same fate.

## RODENTICIDE

Rodenticide is just a fancy name for rat poison, and it will work on mice and rats alike. Remember that this method could mean a dead rat in your wall, which will be very unpleasant for you and your neighbors. Poison is usually an option for people dealing with an outdoor rodent problem, but if you're not having luck with snap traps, poison bait might be worth a try. If you decide go this route, be very careful if you have pets, small children, or are prone to drinking heavily and eating things you find on the ground.

Rodenticide is somewhat controversial. It's highly toxic, but any rodent who eats it could potentially stay alive for a few days after ingesting it. This means that anything that eats the poison rodent will be poisoned, too, including your dear old cat! The use of outdoor rodenticide poses threats to animals like owls, hawks, raccoons, squirrels, deer, and foxes, since any of these animals could ingest it without knowing.

## SOME THINGS TO KNOW IF YOU ARE TRYING TO POISON RATS:

1.    Rats are world-class scavengers, so killing them with poison is more difficult than just putting the poison in their food. Rats will eat a tiny bit of something, and if they don't get sick or suspect foul play, they'll continue eating it. This means any poison you introduce must be completely odorless and

tasteless, and it must have a delayed effect.

2.    Make sure to eliminate all other (nonpoisonous) food supply as much as humanly possible. Nothing will drive a rat from its hole like hunger, and if you leave it no choice it will eventually chow down on the poison.

Rats on the Pill!

New York City has recently introduced birth control bait in hopes of controlling the rat problem. Apparently it sends lady rats into early menopause, which keeps them from having babies. We heard that the city is currently working to figure out which foods are best to bait. But rats eat anything and everything, so we say just shove it in a packet of warm mayonnaise and repeat.

# CHAPTER FOUR:
## BEDBUGS

If you have bedbugs, you're screwed. You should just pack up and move right this instant. They are seriously the worst pest you can have. (We'd rather have rats.) Anyone who's had them will tell you that it is the most horrific experience of their life. Your whole body will be covered in itchy red bites, and you're gonna spend tons of time and money dealing with them.

But before you go breaking your lease, there are some things you can do. Know that you absolutely, positively, MUST call in the pros to treat bedbugs, so if you even *think* you have them, call your landlord. He or she will probably send someone out to inspect and treat your apartment, and most of the time (but not all of the time), they will foot the bill for any costs.

---

"But I have a slumlord! What do I do?!"

It's not uncommon to have never laid eyes on your landlord. Many of us deal strictly with shady management companies who never return our calls, so getting them to drop stacks on expensive pest control treatments is probably out of the question. Have no fear: this is America. The law is on your side.

The first thing you should do is check your lease. Is there anything in writing about pest control? No? That's okay. You still have rights. In most states, landlords and building managers are required to keep their buildings livable and safe. Do a little research and find out what, specifically, your landlord is legally obligated to do or not do. Here in New York, we have the option of employing a nice little legal procedure called repair and deduct. This means if the living conditions in our apartments are dangerous, we can have the problem fixed at our own expense, and then deduct that cost from the rent.

There are rules to the this, though. First off, the problem has to really threaten our health or safety. You can't just play the deduct-and-repair card every time you see a cockroach, but if you have hundreds of them crawling on your face in the middle of the night, you probably can. Second, you must give the landlord notice of the problem and provide him or her access to your apartment. It's always a good idea to get something in writing, so write them and let them know that if they don't take action by a certain date, you will arrange to have it taken care of yourself and will be deducting the cost from next month's rent. And make sure to get a receipt or proof of payment from the exterminator, so the landlord knows you're not just screwing him.

Lastly, you can always look into filing a complaint with your state or local housing board. Here in

New York that's the NYC Department of Housing Preservation and Development (HPD), and filing a complaint with them will get them out to your apartment for an inspection. If they find an infestation or other unlivable conditions, they will issue your landlord a violation and demand that he or she fix the problem within a certain amount of time. If your landlord STILL won't do it, they'll be fined, and it's probably time for you to seriously consider finding yourself a new landlord.

*We're not lawyers. These are simply guidelines to help you (sort of) understand your rights. Don't consider it legal advice. Do your own research before you go suing your landlord or filing complaints with the city.

## Some Basic Bedbug Facts

Bedbugs are found all over the world, NOT just in New York, which comes as a surprise to many paranoid tourists. They were really common pre-WWII, but then the pesticide DDT hit the market and wiped them out. Apparently DDT was fucking up all kinds of other shit, too, like humans and bald eagles, so everyone got all outraged and DDT was banned. Today it's thought that the ban is the reason why bedbugs are back with a vengeance, along with an increase in international travel.

Bedbugs don't care whether you're dirty or clean. Like cockroaches, people think bedbugs prefer filth, but they really will live anywhere. They're more common in areas where animals nest (especially bats), and they thrive in really close quarters, which is probably why everyone always wants to point the finger at New York. They have no trouble traveling through walls and ceilings, so your neighbor's bedbugs could really easily become your bedbugs.

Despite the clever name, they don't just live in beds. They'll live in furniture, clothes, record collections, whatever. They prefer cracks and crannies and heavy upholstery like curtains and rugs. They don't actually build their homes *in* your mattress. They usually live in your bed frame and box springs and come out at night to bite you while you are sleeping, but they can strike in the daytime too. They prefer it if you're passed out, but if they're hungry enough they'll get you while you're awake. Moral of the story and key point to remember: bedbugs do not give a shit.

Bedbugs can lie dormant for about a year without having to eat. They've been known to hang out in vacant apartments, playing dead, waiting to feast on human flesh. The only food they eat is blood. YOUR BLOOD. (Actually, they eat animal blood, too.)

The good news is they aren't known to carry diseases, but most bedbug victims would rather have the bubonic plague than have to live one more day with them.

## How to Tell If You Have Bedbugs

First you have to know what they look like. Just because it is a bug does not mean it is a bedbug. If you think you see one, do your research before you go all crazy and put your house on the market. Maybe you'll get lucky and it will be some other kind of bug living in your bed.

Adult bedbugs are about the size of an appleseed. Their bodies are flat and oval shaped. They are usually brown, but after they've sucked your blood their bodies puff up and turn reddish in color.

If you wake up with a bunch of welts you didn't have the night before, you probably have bedbugs. Bedbugs usually leave a trail of three or four bites in a straight line. The bites might be painless. No two people react the same to bedbug bites. Some turn into welts, some look more like mosquito bites, and some go totally unnoticed.

> "Me and my roommate ripped our apartment to pieces because we thought we found bedbugs. After multiple bags of trash, hours of cleaning, and parting with useless items he and I both find sentimental, the exterminator comes in and tells me 'Oh, that's just a spider beetle. No big deal.' Hey, at least we finally cleaned!"
>
> —JVO, Brooklyn

But most likely in a few days they'll start to itch like hell. You'll probably try to blame it on a mosquito or a flea, but deep down you'll know.

Okay, so if you're seeing bites, take off all your sheets and pillowcases right away. Lift your mattress up and peel back the little strip of fabric that covers your box spring. Check the seams of your mattress, the corners of your headboard, and all other imaginable crevices to see if there are bugs crawling around in there. You should also check out any furniture around your bed, as well as stacks of records, books, or maga-

### Real Bedbug Nightmare

"It was my first Christmas in NYC and I couldn't afford to go home to see my family. I had just moved into a new place (hence the reason I was so very poor), and everyone I knew was gone, including my roommate. On the night before Christmas Eve I found the first row of bites. I had no money and nowhere else to stay, so I had to stick it out. I spent Christmas Day sobbing on the floor in the freezing cold. Oh, I forgot to mention that our heat wasn't working, either."

—LV, Queens

zines. They've also been known to hang out in telephones and radios (although you probably haven't seen either of those things in at least five years). They can live in electrical outlets as well. You'd better just check everything you own.

Other clues besides gross itchy bites:

- blood on your sheets (sick!)
- rust-colored splotches on sheets and mattresses (it's bedbug poop)
- see-through egg sacs or little skin casings (they shed their skin like crazy)
- a "musky" odor (this comes from their scent glands)

If there's anything more disgusting than waking up to a bed full of bedbug skin casings, we haven't found it.

## Takin' Care of Business

If you're sure you have bedbugs, know that it's okay to cry. There's rough road ahead, so let it all out. Now get it together and follow these steps:

1.    Start by washing ALL YOUR LINENS in hot water. We're talking sheets, pillowcases, curtains, rugs, and clothes. Anything that can't be laundered (shoes, stuffed animals, your girlfriend) can be tossed in the dryer. Use the highest dryer setting possible and leave everything in for one to two hours. As soon as they come out, bag them up in airtight plastic bags, and don't take them out until you need to use them.

2.    Take a wire brush and scrub the seams of your mattress. This is supposed to get rid of any egg sacs lying around. Af-

Some Advice from Someone Who's Been There:

"The first rule of bedbugs is you don't talk about bedbugs. Don't go around telling everyone you have them or they'll treat you like a goddamn leper. My friends stopped answering my calls and my girlfriend wouldn't talk to me for a week."
—Anonymous

(Ed note: You should probably not have people over to your house, and you definitely shouldn't sleep anywhere else, but since bedbugs can't jump or fly, your chances of spreading them by shaking hands is pretty slim.)

ter you've done that, vacuum like hell. Like, vacuum the bed itself. Take the vacuum cleaner bag out right away. Put it in the trash outside. Not in your kitchen. Buying or renting a portable steamer is another good option, since you can use it to clean anything that can't be thrown in the washer. Works well on mattress seams, couch cushions or armchairs, and baseboards.

Now take a minute to pat yourself on the back. You're doing really a really good job. You're gonna get through this, but you're not done yet.

4.    Now you have to call an exterminator. There's no way around this one. Bedbugs are really complicated pests. You can't get rid of them all by yourself. This is important: you gotta leave it to the pros. They'll know what kind of treatment is best. Some use heat treatments, some use a cocktail of different poisons. We know following directions totally sucks, but you gotta trust them wholeheartedly. Like Obi-Wan Kenobi, they're your only hope.

Don't start throwing all your crap away just yet.

The exterminator will tell you whether or not that's a good idea, and if you end up needing to throw anything out, they'll help you do it right so you don't get bugs everywhere.

Definitely get a cover for your mattress. These run about thirty bucks, and we know that's, like, really, really expensive, but it's worth it. Get one that's specially made for bedbugs and not one of those cheap ones you buy at the dollar store to prevent pee stains. Now is not the time to cut corners.

Despite what you might have heard, burning your mattress is not an option. We know it sounds like a lot of fun, but it's actually a real pain in the ass. Most mattresses are treated with a fire-retardant chemical, so it probably won't burn all the way and then you'll be left with a scorched hunk of mattress in your yard forever. Plus the cops will probably come and your neighbors will get all pissed off from the smoke. We don't recommend it.

Bedbug-sniffing dogs are all the rage here in New York. For about three hundred bucks you can have a specially trained dog come out and sniff around your apartment. If they smell bedbugs, they'll start pawing and scratching, just like the dogs that find drugs or dead bodies. (Ed note: Unclear whether or not these dogs will be able to find your drugs or dead bodies.) The dogs first arrived on the scene a few years ago during the height of bedbug pandemonium. We think it seems like a big waste of time since all they do is track the scent and not the actual bug. (Lots of times dogs will paw at areas that exterminators find to be totally bug-free.) You're better off just calling a human to come out and take a look.

## Bedbug Do's and Don'ts

The following tips come from bedbugger.com, a resource you should definitely utilize if you're dealing with this nightmare.

- DO catch them, dead or alive. If you're a renter, you can show your landlord and demand justice. Your exterminator is gonna want to see them, too. Catch them with clear packing tape and stick them to an index card. You should also save any skin shedding or egg sacs you find, which is totally gross but definitely necessary.

• DON'T SLEEP SOMEWHERE ELSE. If you have bedbugs or you even *think* you have bedbugs, stay put! You can't just crash on the couch, and you definitely can't stay with someone else. Doing any of these things will just spread them around. Fleeing the country isn't an option, either. They'll be waiting for you when you get back.

• DON'T rule out scabies. You could just have a weird skin condition.

• DON'T TRY TO KILL THEM WITH CHEMICALS. If you start spraying a whole bunch of poison around your house, you could cause them to scatter, which makes it even harder for the exterminator to do his job. They should be the only people spraying poison around.

- DON'T seal up everything just yet. It's okay to wash your clothes and sheets like we said before, but don't go around putting everything you own into plastic bags. The exterminator might want to inspect your stuff, and you could be trapping bugs in instead of keeping them out. Wait and see what the pros say.

- DON'T freak out if they don't go away right away. If after two weeks they're still eating you alive, get another professional treatment. If that still doesn't do it, have them treat it again in another two weeks. Repeat until all signs of evil are gone.

- DO ask questions. What is this poison called? What does it do? Where are you putting it? How long will it take to work? Take notes. If you're not seeing results, hit up bedbugger.com. Lots of other survivors and pest-control professionals read the site regularly, and someone there might be able to offer feedback.

- DO find out if there's anything you can be

doing yourself in between treatments to combat the problem, but remember: the exterminator's word is gospel. Follow his instructions no matter what. Some pros might tell you to vacuum every day, but others might tell you that vacuuming will interfere with their process. Obey them at all costs. (Look, it's not a cult. If you really think you're getting the shaft or that your guy is a total kook, you could get a second opinion. But aren't you stressed out enough already?!)

- And last, but not least: good luck.

---

### Real Bedbug Nightmare

"My girlfriend broke up with me when she found out I had bedbugs. I was crushed at first, but then I found out her next boyfriend gave her crabs. I felt pretty good about that."

—SD, Manhattan

# CHAPTER FIVE:
## ANTS

Ants aren't really all that scary looking. They're kind of cute, actually. But when they gang up, they can be a real pain in the ass, leaving scent trails all over the place and eating up all your plants. Plus, it's gross to have bugs running around your house, no matter how non-threatening they look under a microscope. The trick to getting rid of them is twofold: first, you have to understand how they eat. Second, you have to understand how they socialize.

## Social Lives

There are sixty different kinds of ants in North America. There are different methods for getting rid of different species, but we'll cover methods that will do the job no matter what kind of ants you have.

Let's start with commonalities among the species.

Adult ants cannot consume solid foods. Before they can digest it, they have to turn it into a liquid. So, when they eat a piece of solid food, their insides leak out this digestive juice that breaks it down into a liquid so they can process all those nutrients. Ants also have a little storage space called a *crop* that lets them store pieces of solid food for later when they get the munchies. This is why any store-bought ant killer comes in liquid form. You'll get better results this way than trying to feed them solid poisons.

Ants live in colonies (duh). These can range from a few dozen ants to a few thousand. Ant colonies contain these different types of ants:

- Worker Ants. Worker ants are mostly sterile females that don't have wings. They usually break down into castes, with one group having a higher place in the hierarchy than others.

• Drone Ants. Drone ants are male ants, and they usually have wings. They are the only male ants in the colony. Unlike worker ants, drones contribute absolutely nothing to the colony. They just lay around in their nests.

• Winged Princess Ants. These are winged females who have the ability to get pregnant. Once a year, they all get together for what is called the *nuptial flight*, which is basically a scientific term for an ant orgy. Once they've boned, the male drone ants die and the princess starts searching for a nice spot to lay her eggs. (Probably somewhere under your house.)

• Queen Ants. Queen ants are super badass. They are always grown-ups, and always capable of reproducing, but they don't always have to have sex in order to make babies. That's right! Queen ants do this thing called *asexual parthe-*

*nogenesis*, which is basically cloning yourself. Somehow an unfertilized egg becomes an embryo all on its own, without getting fertilized. There can be more than one queen ant in a colony, and they can live for up to twenty-eight years, which is longer than any other known insect. The only thing that kind of sucks about queen ants is they don't get to boss all the other ants around like the name suggests. They're basically just there to make weird clone babies.

Ants are everywhere! The only ant-free places in the world are Antarctica, the Arctic, and a few tropical islands nobody's ever heard of. Those countries that don't have a native ant species have at

Some species of ants will kidnap other ants' babies and force them into slavery. They'll kill all the adults in a particular nest and abduct the young, forcing the babies to work for their queen and care for their young. Not all of them stand for it. Some captives will rebel later in life by killing the young of their captors, sometimes wiping out as much as two-thirds of the colony!

least one invasive ant species. These little dudes cannot be held down. In the last hundred years, the Argentine ant has made itself at home on SIX different continents. If they can conquer the world in a hundred years, they can do serious damage to your weak ass vegetable garden.

Carpenter ants are the celebrities of the ant world. They are the most common and the most well known. These are the ones you always see in your house or gar-

It's true that ants can lift fifty times their own body weight. That's like a 180 lb dude lifting nine thousand pounds.

den. They build their homes in wood, which usually makes it all weak and flimsy. They can travel as far as one hundred yards to look for food (that's serious distance if you're as small as these guys are). Like every pest ever, they're most active at night.

# On the Hunt!

Here are some places ants like to hang out.

OUTSIDE:

- edge of the foundation or sidewalk
- edge of the driveway
- fences

- edge of the lawn or flower beds
- cracks in the sidewalk
- next to cement blocks or wooden steps
- tree branches that are close to the house
- stump roots near or under the house

INSIDE:

- next to wiring or plumbing
- insulation in wall spaces
- edges of cabinets

Ants are at their busiest between 10 p.m. and 2 a.m. Inclement weather won't stop their party—they'll keep on working through rain or shine. But, if a climate becomes too wet or too dry, they'll move the party indoors.

## Diseases

None! Sometimes they bite and leave little welts (especially fire ants), but they are not known to carry any diseases.

## Remedies!

There are all kinds of natural remedies you can use to wipe out a colony. Before you go out and spend a ton of money on fancy ass ant killers, remember that Windex will do the job just as well. If you're trying to avoid chemicals altogether, there are tons of ways to keep it organic.

Diatomaceous earth works on ants the same way it works on roaches (see page 55). They don't need to eat it because it destroys their exoskeletons. It gets all over their little bodies, and since they won't realize it right away, they'll bring it back to the colony and get it all over their friends.

There are certain lines that ants won't cross. They won't mess around with chalk, Vaseline, chapstick, or talc. If you find an ant hole or a particularly large cluster of ants, draw a line around them with any of these. After you've got them trapped, dump some diatomaceous earth on them. Death is imminent.

We've heard that putting bay leaves in the pantry will keep ants away, but this seems kind of weak.

You can simmer a cinnamon stick if you find ants in your kitchen. The smell drives them away. And your kitchen will smell like Grandma's house at Christmastime! Which is a good thing, unless your grandma is a mean old troll. If you're lazy and you don't feel like simmering anything, just sprinkle some powdered cinnamon around.

> It would take about 450,000 ants to carry a full-grown human.

Lighter fluid is a super hardcore way to deal with an ant problem. It's not a good idea to go around spraying it on every ant you see, but putting a little around the outside frames of doors and windows will keep them away. Don't be an idiot—use it sparingly, and remember, IT'S FLAMMA-BLE!

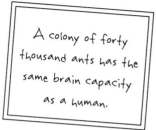

A colony of forty thousand ants has the same brain capacity as a human.

Here is a list of plants and herbs that will repel ants:

- fresh, whole bay leaves
- cloves
- mint leaves (crush 'em up)
- cinnamon
- garlic (also works on vampires)
- pennyroyal
- spearmint
- tansy
- southernwood
- turmeric

Try leaving a slice of watermelon or cantaloupe about one yard from your house. They'll flock to it and leave your kitchen alone.

Ants hate cucumbers. Leave a few cucumber peels (the skin part) on your windowsill to keep them away.

Lavender blossoms near doors and windows will also keep them away, and they smell lovely!

You know that gross peanut brittle your grandmother always sends at Christmas? Set a piece out overnight. Return in the morning to find the entire hunk covered with trapped ants. Rinse those little dudes down the drain. You can reuse it! Thanks, Grandma!

> It's illegal to kill ants in Germany! They're really good for forests since they kill insects that attack trees. You gotta have a permit to kill them, and if you're caught you could face a hefty fine!

Coffee grounds are a good ant repellent, but be careful. Roaches love them.

For anthills in your yard, mix ¼ cup liquid hand soap into a gallon of water. Pour down the hole. Drown those suckers out.

## Spray Solutions

We like spray remedies because they're cheap and easy to make. Most of these oils cost less than ten bucks, and you can get a spray bottle at the dollar store for, like, fifty cents. Added bonus: most of these will leave your home smelling fresh and clean (except for the one that uses horse manure).

• Pine Oil. Pine oil is a very festive way to repel ants. Use it around the holidays and your place will smell like Christmas cheer. Make sure you get the pure pine oil, with no other chemicals added. You only need a little bit—one drop in one quart of water will do the trick.

• Dr. Bronner's Peppermint Soap. Hippies love this shit. It's all-natural, and you can use it for all kinds of things besides cleaning yourself. Mix it up with a little water and spray in problem areas, particularly around baseboards. You can also mix a little bit into your mop water and clean your floors.

• Tobacco. Everyone knows smoking is really cool. But nicotine is poisonous to ants and other insects! Soak one cigarette in one quart of water. Let it stand overnight. In the morning, put some into a spray bottle. (Probably best to use this one outside. It stains, and it doesn't smell great, either.)

• Citrus. Citrus works great as an all-natural ant repeller. Soak lemon peels or orange peels (or both!) in very hot water. Let sit overnight. Pour it into a spray bottle and attack!

• Horse Manure. If you've got a lot of horse shit lying around that you're not sure what to do with, mix it up with some hot water and let it cool. Spray it all around your yard and wait for your neighbors to bitch you out.

• Peppermint Oil. Dilute some pure peppermint oil with water and put the mixture into a spray bottle. (Remember to get the 100 percent pure oil and not the peppermint extract.) Spray it around the outside of your house where the building meets the ground. If you're going to use this in your kitchen, use it sparingly. Nobody wants their bread to taste like a candy cane. Here's a recipe: In a spray bottle, mix ½ teaspoon natural soap (Dr. Bronner's will work) with twelve drops of peppermint oil (NOT the extract!). Add 8 ounces water and shake it like hell. Then spray it around windows, door seals, or any other place you think ants might be coming through.

- Vinegar. Dilute some vinegar with water and spray it anywhere you've seen ants. Vinegar messes with their scent trails, and since they rely on scent to find food (and their way home),

> Ants breathe in unison! Colonies always breathe at the same time, like one big yoga session. Their breathing patterns even stay synched when they are separated from the colony.

they'll avoid it. Clean your counters with it once a week to keep the little turds at bay. (Ed note: This one works on roaches, too!)

- Tea Tree Oil. Something in tea tree oil messes with ants' antennae, leaving them totally confused and disoriented (much like you coming home from the bar at 3 a.m.). They'll avoid it. Here's a recipe: In a spray bottle, mix ½ cup tea tree oil, ¼ cup vinegar, and two cups water together. Spray onto countertops and wipe clean with a damp paper towel or dish rag. (Ed note: This one works on roaches, too!)

## Ant-Repelling Recipes

If you like to cook, there are all kinds of recipes you can make that will get rid of ants. Any of these will seem like a delicious treat to the ant, and they'll swarm on it and gobble it all up. Worker ants are devoted slaves who are very good at sharing, so once they get back to the colony, they'll share their treats with the rest of the colony (suckers!).

SUGAR OVERDOSE

¼ cup honey

¼ cup sugar

¼ cup borax (about half that if you're using 100 percent boric acid)

Mix up the honey and sugar. Microwave it for one minute. After it gets liquidy, add in the borax and stir well. Put a little in areas where ants hang out, but it's sticky (duh) so you probably don't want to slather it all over your countertops.

### YEAST INFECTION

6 tbsp granulated sugar

6 tbsp fresh, active dry yeast (you can get this at the grocery store)

½ cup standard grade molasses or honey

10 plastic bottle caps (metal caps will work, too)

Mix all ingredients in a small bowl until smooth. Put a little bit in each bottle cap. Leave near ant mounds or trails.

### HONEYSUCKER

½ tsp boric acid

½ tsp honey

Mix together and place in a shallow dish. Leave out overnight.

### CAP IN THE ASS

1 cup sugar

3 tbsp boric acid

3 cups warm water

plastic bottle caps

Mix the sugar and boric acid together, then slowly add warm water. Stir constantly so the mixture does not get lumpy. Pour some into the bottle caps and soak a cotton ball in there.

### THE BLACK (PEPPER) DEATH

1 cup borax (about half if you're using pure boric acid. See page 52 for warnings/where to buy)

¼ cup crushed, fresh black pepper

¼ cup crushed bay leaves

Mix ingredients in a jar and shake it like a salt shaker. Sprinkle on problem areas. (This one works on roaches, too!)

## SUGAR COMA

¼ cup sugar

¼ cup baking yeast

½ cup molasses

Six 3 x 5-inch index cards

Mix all ingredients together in a bowl. Use a knife to spread it all over the index cards in thin layers. Leave the cards anywhere you've seen ants. They'll get stuck in the sweet, sugary goodness.

## CAYENNE ASSASSIN

¼ lb dried peppermint (you can get it at the health food store, probably the farmers market, too.)

¼ lb rock dust (nursery)

¼ lb seaweed powder (garden supply)

¼ lb alfalfa meal (health food store)

¼ lb cayenne pepper

Put all this stuff into a bowl and mix well. Don't get any on your hands, and definitely don't get any in your eyes. (The cayenne pepper will melt your face off.) Sprinkle a little bit where you've seen ants.

OFF WITH HER HEAD!

Killing the queen is the best way to take out an ant colony. Without their queen, the colony gets all pathetic and weak. Not as many babies are born without her, so theoretically the colony will die out over time. (The toughest colonies have more than one queen.)

These two recipes are specially formulated to target the queen:

1 tbsp grape jelly

¼ tsp boric acid

½ tsp wet cat food (The cheap stuff will do. No need to splurge on that Fancy Feast.)

Using gloves, roll up the mixture into a little ball. Put it where ants can easily get to it. This treat is too big for the worker ants, but they'll break it down and take it back to their queen as an offering. She'll gorge herself on it, and she'll croak not too long after.

This one works in the same way:

1 part baking soda

1 part powdered sugar

1 tsp powdered vitamin C

½ tsp diatomaceous earth

½ tsp honey

Roll this one into little balls, too. Wait for the swarm.

# CHAPTER SIX:
# ASSORTED PESTS

There are all kinds of weird creatures that could crawl into your house. This chapter talks about some of the more common kinds we've seen.

We recently learned that there is such a thing as a handheld electric bug zapper! It's shaped like a tennis racket, and when you press a button it emits a little electrical charge that stuns tiny critters. It's really fun to play with, and it does the job.

# Centipedes and Millipedes

Everyone always wants to group these two into the same category, but centipedes and millipedes are two different beasts SO GET IT RIGHT!

| CENTIPEDES | MILLEPEDES |
| --- | --- |
| Freakishly long legs that extend far out from their bodies | Short, stumpy legs |
| Long antennae | Teeny antennae that you can't see from far away |
| Really fast runners | Slow walkers |
| THEY BITE | Don't bite |
| THEY ARE PREDATORS (they hunt) | Don't hunt (they scavenge) |

Both are arthropods, which is like, a cousin of insects. Let's start with the grosser one.

## CENTIPEDES

*Centipede* means "one hundred legs," but an adult centipede can have anywhere from fifteen to 177 *pairs* of legs. Sometimes their legs are really thick and hairy, and sometimes they are dainty and delicate, like a ballerina or a fashion model. It depends on the species. If one pair of legs gets ripped off, another can grow back in its place. Most of them

> Centipedes can change color to camouflage themselves against predators. They also might change color if they get pissed off or scared.

are reddish brown in color. They can get as big as five inches long and live for up to five years.

Centipedes have really sensitive antennae. They use them for hunting prey, as well as sensing vibrations and maybe even hearing (jury's still out on whether they can hear or not). Their mouths are teeny tiny, but they have these vicious, claw-like jaws that have poison in them. The poison paralyzes their victims (worms, spiders, and other small insects), which makes it easy for them to chow down.

Centipedes are fierce hunters, but they won't bite humans unless they're provoked, so don't go around fondling them. Even though they're poisonous, you probably won't die if you get bit by one, but it can sort of mess you up. Symptoms include severe pain (the bigger the centipede, the worse the pain), swelling, redness, itchiness, swollen lymph nodes, headaches, heart palpations or a racing pulse, nausea, vomiting, and anxiety. The bites of giant, monster-like centipedes can send humans into anaphylactic shock, which is just, like, a serious allergic reaction where everything swells up and you can't breathe. Small children and feeble people are more sensitive to centipede bites, as well as those with known insect allergies.

The bite will look different than a spider bite, like two little claw marks instead of two round dots. If you think one got you and you have any of these symptoms, call a doctor.

Most species of centipede prefer the outdoors. They

like moist, dark, secluded areas. The house centipede is the only species that
is capable of reproducing indoors, so if you see one inside,
it's probably this kind. House
centipedes hide during the
daytime and roam around at
night, probably in your bath-

Centipedes are cannibals. They'll eat other centipedes and show no remorse. Vicious!

room, closet, or basement, since that's where they
have the most luck finding prey.

## MILLIPEDES

*Millipede* means "a thousand legs," but remember
that they are slow-moving scavengers. They feed on
rotten leaves and decomposing wood, so they're almost always outside. They do tend to migrate in the
fall, probably looking for a place to hang out for the
winter. This is when you're most likely to see them
in your home. They'll also try to get in if the weather
gets too wet outside. They like damp areas, but they
don't want to drown.

You'll probably find millipedes in the same indoor spots you find centipedes: basements, bathrooms, and crawlspaces. The good news is they usually starve to death within a few days once they're indoors, unless you have piles of dead leaves laying around for them to feed on.

Some species of millipedes have glands that will secrete toxic liquids when they feel threatened. Some of them can even squirt this stuff up to several inches away, and it smells totally foul. The toxin may cause an allergic reaction in some people, known as a "millipede burn." This stuff is extra nasty if it gets in your eyes, even causing blindness in some cases, but that's pretty rare. Mostly it will just make your eyelids swell up. If you're holding a millipede and it squirts you, ask yourself why you are holding a millipede in the first place. Your skin will probably turn brown, and this stain can last for months! If the area starts burning or itching really bad or you develop blisters, call a doctor, especially if you've gotten any in your eyes.

## HOW TO GET RID OF THEM

Your chances of getting totally overrun by cen-tipedes or millipedes is pretty slim since they're mostly outdoor creatures, but if you're seeing a ton of them in your house, you've got problems. (Not everyone would agree that a house full of centipedes is a bad thing. Like spiders, they kill a lot of bugs, and apologists argue that hav-ing them around means you won't see many other kinds of bugs in your house. But they're disgusting looking. So they gotta go.)

Unfortunately, there ar-en't that many cool ways to kill either of these dudes. Boric acid will work in the same way it works for roaches (see page 52), but it's harder to bait centipedes because they're carnivores. And also because it can be hard-er to tell where they're coming from since they only come out at night.

> "Febreeze will kill bugs. One ran up my ceiling and thought he was safe. Nope. Sprayed the hell out of him." —KK, Brooklyn

If you're seeing tons of either of these guys in your house, your DIY options are pretty slim.

•   Stomp 'em Out. Step on them. Hit them with a flyswatter. For bathroom visitors, use you roommate's shampoo bottle. With centipedes you gotta move quick! These guys are speed demons. Turn your back for one second and they'll be gone.

•   Sticky Traps. Sticky traps will catch any insect that crawls on them. They also give you a good indication of how many other kinds of creatures you have crawling around. If you wake up in the morning and find six hundred dead bugs stuck to your trap, call in the pros. Boric acid is useless to you at that point.

•   Keepin' it Dry. Both centipedes and millipedes seek out places that are damp and dingy, like basements and bathrooms. Get a dehumidifier. They're expensive, but they're good for you. They'll help keep your place from getting all moldy, and they're good for allergies, too.

- Seal it Up. Seal off cracks and holes with some of that trusty old caulk we talked about on page 49. These guys like the outdoors more than your basement, anyway. If they can't get in they'll just say fuck it and leave it alone.

- Spray 'em with Poison. Buy some spray. Spray it on them.

That's it! Good luck!

# Fruit Flies

Fruit flies don't really cause any serious damage, but they're a real pain in the ass. One day one makes his home in your fruit bowl, and the next day all his buddies are swarming. And produce is expensive, man! You can't have bugs crawling all over your six dollar bag of grapes. Luckily, fruit flies are pretty easy to take out if you know how to exploit their weaknesses.

## FRUIT FLIES VS. GNATS

Lots of people think they have fruit flies when they really have gnats. Gnats are really small, like little black flying specks. Fruit flies are really small, too, but they actually *look* like flies and not little dots with wings.

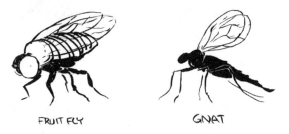

FRUIT FLY                    GNAT

Fruit flies want your fruit (no surprise there). They are really bad sugar addicts, and when your fruit starts to rot, they freak out and swarm all over it. So keep it stored in the fridge. You can cover stuff you don't want to refrigerate (peaches, tomatoes) with a lightweight linen cloth, or maybe a piece of cheesecloth. This keeps fruit flies from laying their eggs in your overpriced organic produce.

It's also a good idea to wash ALL your fruit (yes, even oranges and bananas) as soon as you bring it home. Keeping your sink free of dirty dishes always helps, and it never hurts to dump a cup of bleach or some boiling water down the drain every month or so. Also, get a lid for your trash can, and make sure you rinse out any food or drink container that you recycle or throw away.

Fruit flies love getting drunk. Always rinse out your beer cans or wine bottles before you recycle them, and make sure to do a good job cleaning up after a rager.

You can trap fruit flies with a plastic bottle (an empty, clean, one-liter or two-liter will work) and a funnel. No need to buy one—you can make one by rolling up a sheet of notebook paper. Use either of these mixtures to bait them:

"My one friend makes us rinse out our empties every time we go over there to drink. It's really annoying. No one wants to go over there to party anymore. But not because of the fruit flies."
—LV, Queens

Pour ½ cup apple cider vinegar and a few drops of dish soap into the plastic bottle. Insert the funnel. Fruit flies will crawl down in but won't be able to get out.

You can also use booze, but who would waste it?! Pour ½ cup of beer or sweet white wine into your bottle (we've also heard tequila will work). Throw in a couple chunks of fruit (it doesn't matter what kind). Insert the funnel and wait for your fruit fly collection to grow.

"Fruit flies? I just eat a few of them. Like, suck them right out of the air. The rest of them will think you are Godzilla, and they'll fly away and never return."
—DK, New Jersey

If you find the funnel isn't cutting it, try this trap: fill a juice glass halfway with cider vinegar. Add two teaspoons of dishwashing liquid. Cover that baby up with plastic wrap and secure it with a rubber band. Use a fork to poke a few holes in the top. They'll get trapped in there and die a vinegary death.

Another good jar trick is the ol' piece of rotten fruit in a mason jar. Anything that is just a little bit past ripe will do. (We like peaches.) Once it's kind of rotten, throw it in the jar and cover it up with plastic wrap. Then cover it with a rubber band and poke those fork holes. Those little freaks will swarm to it right before your eyes. Then you can dump 'em down the drain or release them outside. Make sure you change the fruit on the regular. You don't want it getting *too* rotten.

> Tip! Dishwashing liquid makes it really hard for fruit flies to fly because it weighs down their wings. Throw a couple drops in any of these remedies to really amp up the attack.

Any can of cheap beer will work as a fruit fly trap. Don't open it all the way: just pop the top so there's a little crack for the fruit flies to get in. (If you mess up, just chug it then get a new one.) They really like beer, and they'll crawl down in there and get too wasted to get out. (We've all been there.) Let the can sit for twenty-four hours. When you throw it out, do it away from your kitchen. Use your outside trash can or your neighbor's yard.

Another method is to nuke them in the microwave. Put any leftover fruit in the microwave and leave the door open. Once there are lots of them in there, shut the door and turn it on. A minute should do it.

Cooked potato peels will work as bait, too. Use them to bait the little dudes into the microwave, or wait until they swarm all over the peels and then spray them with poison.

If you have a dishwasher, you are probably rich! You can use this modern convenience to catch fruit flies. Load it up with dirty dishes, then put the soap in like usual. Pour ¼ cup of cider vinegar in the bottom of the machine. Leave the door open for about an hour, then close it and run that sucker. You'll drown them all and wash them down the drain.

You can also zap them with a blowtorch.

You can also buy store-bought traps, but it seems

> They actually sell hats with fly traps attached to them. We have no idea where to buy them (probably the same place you'd buy a full-body camouflage suit), but you could easily make your own by sticking some fly strips to your head. Then just walk around your kitchen a few times really fast.

like a waste of money. They're like ten bucks, and they work almost the exact same way as homemade traps do. They basically just look like fake pieces of fruit, and they come with some pre-fab bait. We say save your money and just leave some beer out. (For ten bucks you can get a lot of beer, and then you can get drunk while you kill them!)

## Spiders!

There are about forty thousand different kinds of spiders worldwide. They're carnivores, but contrary to popular belief, they are not all blood-thirsty monsters trying to feast on your flesh. Like centipedes, some people say that spiders are very good to have in your house because they eat other bugs. But we think they're terrifying.

One spider will eat about a hundred bugs each year. They kill more bugs than birds do. One source claimed that if you were to add up the weight of all the bugs eaten by all the spiders in the world in one day, it would weigh more than all the humans on Earth.

There's a rumor that you are never more than twelve feet away from a spider. This is very unsettling, but there are only four types of poisonous spiders in the United States: the black widow, the brown recluse, the hobo, and the yellow sac spider. Here's where they live, and what to do if you get bitten by one. (Short answer: call a doctor.)

## BLACK WIDOW SPIDER

Black widows live just about everywhere, but they're most common in the southwestern areas of the United States. These are the jet-black ones with the bright red marks on their butts. They like dark, damp places like storage sheds and old woodpiles. You'll know if you've been bitten by one because it will swell up and get really, really painful. Also you might get nauseous and start puking a lot. People rarely die from black widow bites, so wash the bite with soap and water, put some ice on it, and then elevate the area if you can (this keeps the venom from spreading). After that, call a doctor. He or she will give you some drugs.

## BROWN RECLUSE SPIDER

Brown recluse spiders can be found in the Midwest, and also down south. They're skinny and brown and they've got a violin-shaped pattern on their heads, but who's really getting close enough to identify it? They really, really like to hang out by themselves, so they tend to live in dark places that haven't been disturbed in a long time. They can't bite humans without some sort of counter pressure, meaning you'd have to get smashed up against one in order to get bit. If they do bite you, you'll get a little white blister. Then the skin around it will start to turn bluish-black and eventually get all crusty, like a scab. If that happens and you haven't already gone to the doctor, GO NOW. Brown recluse bites will rot your flesh. The doc will give you some medicine and you'll probably be okay, but if you let it get too nasty you might end up needing a skin graft (ew).

## HOBO SPIDER

Hobo spiders live in the Pacific Northwest. They're big and brown with a bright yellow pattern on their bellies. Their webs look like funnels, and they build them in holes and cracks. Like with all the other poisonous spiders, a hobo spider bite will start to look angry and hurt really bad. Call the doctor. If left untreated, a hobo spider bite will get real nasty. It will rot your flesh like a brown recluse bite, and you'll eventually start bleeding out of your orifices. Back in the '80s, some lady in Washington state straight up died of internal bleeding from a hobo bite.

## YELLOW SAC SPIDER

Yellow sac spider bites are the most common of all the poisonous spider bites. They're usually light yellow or pale yellowish-green, and they're huge. They can be found all across the United States, but they're most common in the Pacific Northwest. They usually live outside, but they'll come indoors if they can't find anything to eat. Symptoms of a yellow sac spider bite are a lot like the symptoms of a brown recluse bite or a hobo bite, but they're generally not as severe. In addition to an angry-looking bite, you'll probably get nauseous, develop a fever, and lose your appetite. You might go into shock. Good news: those symptoms are pretty rare. Most of the time a yellow sac bite leaves an itchy bump that goes away in a few days. Still, if the bite starts to look nasty, call a doctor.

Spiders use their eight legs for hearing, feeling, touching, and tasting. Not all of them have eight eyes, but those that do use them all. This doesn't mean they have 20/20 vision. They usually see the world in shapes and shadows instead of clear-cut images.

KILLIN' SPIDERS

- If you want to kill them, spray them with soapy water. All-natural soaps work well, as well as soaps that contain pyrethrum. Dr. Bronner's Peppermint Soap is a good choice.

- Raid works. We like this method because you can stand way back while you spray them (most of those store-bought poisons have a real trajectory on them!), but then you have to watch it wiggle around, which can be unnerving. Make sure you get the kind that's specially formulated for spiders. The roach poison won't work on them.

- Smash them with a shoe. An age-old, tried-and-true method.

## KEEPING IT SPIDER-FREE

Get out the caulk! Like with other pests, sealing cracks and entryways is a good start. Doesn't hurt to spray a little poison in there before you seal it up.

Keep outdoor lights off as much as possible. Spiders aren't drawn to light, but the bugs they eat are, and spiders will typically set up shop in places where the hunting is good. It helps to dust or vacuum any webs that form around these areas, too.

We think that glue traps are a terrible way to solve your mouse problem, but they work great for spiders. Leave them in spidery areas. This will get any that crawl on the ground, but the web-builders tend to hang out on the ceiling and probably won't fall victim to these traps.

Hedge apples have been used as crawling insect repellant for hundreds of years. These are the lumpy green balls you always see in the road during summertime. (We call them "monkey balls!") Put them around your house where you usually see spiders. Throw them away before they rot and turn to mush.

"One time I saw a dinosaur-sized spider in the tub. My boyfriend wasn't home to kill it, so I ran out of the bathroom as fast as I could, stuffed some towels under the door so the dino couldn't get out and eat me, then went to the living room and waited for bf to get home and kill it. He got home about 40 minutes later, and when he saw that the water was on he FREAKED OUT, asked me if I was a 'fucking idiot,' and then shut the water off. Of course the dinosaur spider was nowhere to be found, and my boyfriend didn't speak to me for, like, two days after that." —TM, Ohio

If you want to be spider-free and also look like a total psycho, put some wood chips in some old pantyhose and hang them around your house. Spiders will avoid the wood chips.

Chestnuts are an ancient spider remedy. Use fresh chestnuts, not the packaged kind. Put them near doors and cracks. Walnuts will work, too, and so will horse chestnuts. Apparently these give off a smell that spiders really hate, so you can poke some holes in them if you want.

Diatomaceous earth will kill spiders the same way it kills roaches and ants—by cutting them up and leaving them dehydrated (see page 55). This one's good for indoor or outdoor use.

Any of these essential oils can be used against spiders. (You can also see page 28 for other types of oil, and remember that these will work against other insects, too!)

- citronella oil
- lavender oil
- cinnamon oil

- peppermint oil
- citrus oil
- tea tree oil (Careful! It's poisonous to cats and dogs.)

Mix five to six drops of any of these with a teaspoon of dish soap and half a quart of water. Spray away! Reapply once a week.

Spiders hate citrus. We recommend sugar-free 100 percent lemon juice because you can spray it directly on countertops, inside drawers and cabinets, or along doorways and windowsills. MAKE SURE IT'S SUGAR FREE or you will make a sticky mess and probably attract other kinds of hungry pests. You can also leave out lemon, orange, or lime peels, but be careful of fruit flies.

Dust your windowsills with Lemon Pledge. Spiders hate the taste of it, and since their taste buds are in their legs they won't come near it. (We are curious to know who discovered this one. Does this mean that someone somewhere is doing research on what kinds of tastes spiders prefer? Science, man! It's wild!)

RECIPES TO KEEP SPIDERS AWAY

There are a few recipes you can make at home to keep spiders away. These work as spray solutions, and they're cheap and easy to make.

• Mix ¼ cup white vinegar with water. Add a teaspoon of coconut oil. Spray in corners.

• Mix one ounce table salt in one gallon warm tap water. Spray it around, but keep it away from your plants (it will kill them, but if you're anything like us you can't keep houseplants alive anyway).

• Yet another use for tobacco! Buy one package of pipe or chewing tobacco. Boil it in a gallon of water and let it cool. Strain the liquid into a clean container. Mix one cup of the tobacco juice with ½ cup lemon dish soap. Spray like hell. We recommend using this one outdoors unless you want tobacco stains all over your house.

Some people swear that cigarette smoke keeps spiders away. Tell that to your roommate next time she bitches at you for smoking inside.

- Try this one if you like it spicy! You'll need:
  1 cup white vinegar
  2 tbsp chili powder or hot chili sauce
  1 qt water

Pour it all into a spray bottle. Shake it up really well to mix. Spray it anywhere spiders build their webs. (Probably best out of reach of pets and kids. It'll burn ya!)

# RECIPES

Times are tough, man. If you're sick of eating ramen for every meal, why not spice it up and cook up your kill! Here are some thrifty recipes you can whip up on the go.*

## Stir-Fried Cockroaches

Ingredients:
- 4 or 5 cockroaches (recently frozen)
- 1 onion
- 1 red pepper
- 1 green pepper
- 1 tbsp salt

*Editor's note: Don't actually cook anything you kill in your house. Or out of your house, for that matter. These are joke recipes, but you can always substitute chicken or something!

1 tbsp corn starch

4 tbsp cooking oil

2 cups rice

1.     Remove and discard the solid wing covering flaps and all legs of the cockroaches.

2.     Put the cockroaches into a pot of boiling oil and quickly fry for fifteen seconds.

3.     Heat a wok until hot. Add four spoons of oil and put all vegetables into it. Stir-fry for three minutes.

4.     Put the half-cooked cockroaches in the wok. Add salt and corn starch.

5.     Serve on a bed of white rice.

## Barbeque Miceburgers

Ingredients:

100 g of minced mice meat (about 4 or 5 mice)

1 onion

salt and pepper (to taste)

bbq dry rub

1 egg

1 tsp olive oil

soy sauce or Worcester sauce

garlic (for keeping vampires away)

1. Sauté the onion in one teaspoon of olive oil.

2. Mix it with the mouse meat, egg, and dry rub. Add soy sauce or Worcester sauce if you have any, and salt and pepper to taste. (If you like things spicy, kick it up with Tabasco sauce! )

3. Make into patties. Cook like you would a normal burger, about fifteen to twenty-five minutes depending on how you like it.

   Miceburgers are traditionally served on a toasted bun with your favorite toppings.

## Stuffed Porcupine Peppers

Ingredients:

1 red or green pepper per person

1 onion (chopped finely)

1 cup cooked brown rice

1 lb porcupine meat

olive oil for frying

1.    Lightly fry the porcupine in the olive oil.

2.    Add brown rice and onion and cook until soft.

3.    Mix with the porcupine meat. This will be your stuffing.

4.    Decapitate peppers, removing the pips and the white pith membranes. Grill for three minutes.

5.    Add stuffing and heat thoroughly until done. The peppers should be crunchy, not soft and wet. For added heat, use Tabasco sauce.

## Raccoon Stew in a Bread Bowl

Ingredients:

1 raccoon, cleaned, skinned and quartered

4 cups water

2 carrots, diced

1 stalk celery, diced

2 large potatoes, cubed

salt and pepper to taste

one large bread roll, hollowed out

1.     Place the raccoon in a large pot and cover with water. Bring to a boil and cook for one hour.

2.     Remove meat and allow to cool. Drain.

3.     Remove meat from bones and cut into one- to two-inch cubes. Sprinkle with salt and pepper.

4.     Add meat back to pot and add fresh water, carrots, celery, and potatoes. Season to taste with more salt. Bring to a boil, reduce heat, and cook until veggies are tender. Adjust seasoning if needed.

5.     Serve in a bread bowl.

## How to Skin Your Kill:

First, rinse the animal in water. Make sure the little guy is totally saturated. The skin should be completely soaked. This will keep the hair clumped together, which helps with skinning the animal.

Next, use a sharp knife to take out the inner organs. Cut the belly just under the ribs, through the abdomen, and toward the hindquarters. Always remove the bladder first, and be careful not to spill any urine on the meat. Open the pelvis and take out the remaining organs with care and caution.

Next, skin the animal by slicing very close to the skin, from the hind end and over the belly to the animal's flanks. Once that is finished, take the tail and gently but firmly pull toward the forelegs. This will remove the hide.

Finally, the best part: cut off the animal's feet and head. Pull the remaining skin from the legs. Make sure to remove the innards as soon as possible.

Helpful pointer: meat that marinates in the innards will taste gamey.

# INDEX

# Y

# THANK YOUS

## Caroline's Thank Yous

I need to thank a lot of people. Bear with me.

Mom and Dad, you're the coolest. I love you both immensely. Jed, you fucking homeowner. I knew you'd bring your mad genius. (Special shoutouts to Marseille and Iggy for putting up with us.) Thanks to MG for the mgs. Thanks to Zach Gajewski for reading the very first draft of this piece of shit. Kohle, thank you for bringing me to New York, and for always feeding me and getting me high. You truly are a comedic genius ❤ Jim, you are a super cool dude and a total babe. Colin, ur G.O.A.T., bro. Taylor, baby girl, I love you dearly. You are my sister from another mister ❤ Thanks to all my Skyhorse peeps who read later drafts: Jason Katzman, Cory Allyn, and Kristin Kulsavage. Thanks to Danielle Ceccolini for the kickass cover! Katie Kervin, your edits were SUPER helpful. I owe you one free night of Jesus-watching. A very heartfelt thanks to Pat Beauchamp who read this thing more closely than anyone ever should have. Thanks to Sarah Beauchamp for her notes, and the beer she bought me on Saturday after I officially finished this goddamn thing. Thank you to the good people of Reddit, and to everyone else who helped turn this turd into chrome.

I would be lost without you all.

## Jed's Thank Yous

Thank you Marseille and Ignatius for being nice to me while I was drawing this book. Thanks Caroline for picking me to draw it! Thanks Chris Monday, and everyone else I sent drawings to for feedback.

Caroline

Jed

(Friends since 2006)